ST MARTIN'S
TRUE CRIME
CLASSICS

"PLEASE! PLEASE LET ME OUT OF HERE!"

The screams and moans coming from that closet soon became like audible wallpaper in the Knorr household. No one seemed to notice the sounds, but then Theresa Knorr had insisted on stuffing towels underneath the door to the closet so that it muffled her daughter's cries for help. No one seemed concerned about Sheila, except Terry, by now fourteen years of age.

She strained her ears to listen to any telltale signs of her sister's condition inside that small closet. A few days after she was locked in there for the second time, Terry heard Sheila rustling around, desperately peeling off her clothes because of the sweltering eighty-five degree heat that drifted through the day and much of the night.

Sheila would never leave the closet again . . .

St. Martin's Paperbacks True Crime Library
Titles by Wensley Clarkson

Doctors of Death
Whatever Mother Says
Deadly Seduction
Death at Every Stop
In the Name of Satan
Caged Head
The Railroad Killer
The Mother's Day Murder
Slave Girls
The Good Doctor

Whatever Mother Says...

An incredible true story of
death and destruction
inside one ordinary family

Wensley Clarkson

St. Martin's Paperbacks

WHATEVER MOTHER SAYS...

Copyright © 1995 by Wensley Clarkson.

Cover photograph of grave courtesy Superstock, Inc.
Photographs of Teresa Knorr by Pat Thatcher.

ISBN: 978-1-250-09286-1

St. Martin's Paperbacks edition / March 1995

P1

To Clare,
for putting up with me, as usual

Notes of Gratitude

The idea of using a leaden, dispassionate word like "Acknowledgments" for this section cannot begin to express the depth of my feelings for the many individuals who have made this book possible. I owe them my deepest and most heartfelt gratitude.

First to my agent Peter Miller and my editor Charles Spicer. Without them this book would never have happened. Their support and guidance has been very much appreciated.

Then there is: Mark Sandelson, Bud Sullivan, Keith Bendixen, Hal and Fran Cheney, Detective David Lundberg, Pat and Vere Thatcher, Peter Rosen, Ann Cristoferson, Heidi Sorenson, Inspector Johnnie Smith, DeLois Knorr, Robert Knorr Sr., Mickey Sampson, John Trumbo, Sheriff Donald J. Nunes, *L.A. Times* contributor James G. Wright, and Sean Martin.

But my biggest debt of gratitude must go to Sgt. John Fitzgerald—without his help this book would never have been possible.

Author's Note

The central figure in this story, Theresa Jimmie Knorr, changed her name frequently. In an effort to avoid confusion, throughout the book she is referred to by whichever name she was using at the time.

Quotations from written material appears, with few exceptions, without the editorial "[sic]." When it seems that a word was inadvertently missing, it has been added for the sake of clarity. Mistakes in punctuation, grammar, and spelling have been corrected in certain instances, but in others it was felt that retaining an error helped convey the flavor of a document and the style of the person being quoted.

Introduction

As an author and former crime reporter, I have written about many of the most notorious criminals of modern times, from the appalling killings committed by Charles Manson and his flock of disciples to the ultimate crime of passion that made Betty Broderick one of the most infamous murderesses of modern times.

However, I will never forget my response as a parent when I first became aware of the murders allegedly committed by the mother and her two sons featured in this book. How could a mother kill her own flesh and blood? Even worse, how could a woman defy that special bond that is supposed to exist between mother and daughter?

But then mother love can take many forms: hatred, derision, sympathy, inspiration, devotion, self-sacrifice, companionship, destruction, jealousy, admiration, affection, desolation, and, it now seems, even murder.

Mother love is supposed to mean love of a mother for her children. It is a two-way process, which means that the child gradually rises until she is in the ascendent—the succorer, not the succored. Your mother is your mother for always. Your one and only mother. Your mother for all time. You cannot divorce your mother, and if you happen to be her daughter, you are the same sex as her, out of the same mold. It is like a series of those Russian wooden dolls, the sort that fit inside each other, painted with different floral dresses, but shaped the same and becoming smaller and smaller.

Men may rule the genealogical tree, but it is the female side of the family that has a truer inheritance. When a woman has a baby, it is her mother, not her father, she turns to, and if that baby is a girl, in due time she will turn to her mother. That is a real family tree. The family tree of women.

It may be significant that the mother described in this book lost her own mother at a young age. She had no one to turn to at the start of parenthood. No one to guide her. No one to tell her how to do it.

As I began to investigate the circumstances behind the alleged crimes featured in this book, I uncovered such a vast nest egg of hidden abuse that one cannot help asking the question over and over again: Why? The blatant violence committed in the name of the family cannot all have been a thoughtless act. What hidden factors contributed to this tragedy? Why did authorities ignore the pleas of help by one sister and force her back into that house of horrors, and in effect sentence her to death? Why did so many not believe the only surviving daughter when she told authorities what had happened inside that household?

I make no specific stance in presenting the facts in this book as they have been revealed to me through painstaking research and extraordinary access to tape-recorded statements made to investigators during the course of their inquiries, as well as dozens of interviews. I have simply recalled them as they have been recounted by everyone involved.

The actual date of the trial of Theresa Jimmie Knorr and her sons has yet to be confirmed. In the interests of justice, I have been careful not to veer away from the story as it unfolded, according to the many family members, friends, and officials involved.

But if ever a case deserved to be publicized, even in advance of a court case, then this is it. The very fabric of the American family unit is already under enough severe pressure. The story of the Knorrs is a warning of just how bad things can get and why all of us, as responsible adults, have a duty to our children to do something to arrest the decline before it is too late.

It is hardly as if the warnings have not been made in the past. So-called experts have been telling us for years of childhood abuse and its terrifying aftermath.

The battered child syndrome has been described as unrecognized trauma by radiologists, orthopedists, pediatricians, and social workers. It is a significant cause of childhood disability and death.

Unfortunately, it is frequently not recognized, or, if diagnosed, is inadequately handled by physicians because of hesitation to bring the case to the proper authorities.

Yet, incredibly, not so long ago in Western society, unbridled parental domination was an enduring tradition whose roots were seen in the Old Testament.

Later generations took this biblical command quite

literally. Under the Old English common law, children were regarded as the property of their fathers. Parents could require their children to work for them, or place them in indentured servitude in return for payment. Absolute obedience was not an issue—for children who attempted to rebel were whipped and beaten or placed in workhouses.

The harsh treatment of children went hand in hand with prevailing moral and religious beliefs that "childhood was an inherently evil state." This tradition carried over to our own shores where, in 1646 in the Massachusetts Bay Colony, newly arrived citizens (ironically, escaping repression) enacted the Massachusetts Stubborn Child Law. Parents who claimed that their children were "stubborn and rebellious" and "disobedient of voice" could seek one of several "state reprimands," including execution. Obviously, democracy and due process were not things the Pilgrims wanted in their homes.

Children universally attach themselves to their care givers. This is a survival mechanism necessary to provide the needs that a child is unable to satisfy alone. Certainty of the presence of a safe base allows for normal emotional and cognitive development. . . . In the absence of such a safe base, as in cases of child abuse and neglect, a child goes through a variety of psychological maneuvers to preserve maximum protection. Abused and neglected children often become fearfully and hungrily attached to their care givers, with timid obedience and an apparent preoccupation with the anticipation and prevention of abandonment.

In his book, *Soul Murder,* Albert Shengold went so

far as to say that what he described as soul murder was "the deliberate attempt to eradicate or compromise the separate identity of another person. The victims of soul murder remain in large part possessed by another, their souls in bondage to someone else . . . Torture and deprivation under conditions of complete dependency have elicited a terrible and terrifying combination of helplessness and rage—unbearable feelings that must be suppressed for the victim to survive."

When a child is punished severely and unfairly, it becomes a mind-splitting or mind-fragmenting operation because many children have to keep in some compartment of their minds the delusion of good parents and the delusive promise that all terror, pain, and hate will be transformed into love.

Prologue

In October 1993 one of the most disturbing allegations of multiple child abuse ever seen was uncovered thanks to the dogged efforts of one detective and the young woman who claims she narrowly escaped with her life after witnessing a catalogue of terror inside her own family home.

It all began almost ten years earlier in a desolate area of forest near the High Sierra Mountains, in central California. It is a bleak expanse of rugged terrain—the perfect dumping ground for a thousand secrets. A place where a bear or a mountain lion is more likely to come across any human remains than a deputy sheriff or a forest ranger. Nobody knows how many bodies are out there. It is pure luck if anyone stumbles upon them.

And even when human remains are discovered, chances are that those murderers will never be arrested. Usually, the bodies are not even identified. The cops who patrol the area call them body dumps, and over the years they've included every type of death: decapitations, burned-out cars, strangulation, emasculation, impaling; a few had been injected with battery acid, and then there are the ones who've simply been tossed down ravines.

Even when these tragic victims are found, they all too often end up being buried in an unmarked grave with just the name "Jane Doe" on a tiny headstone. Unclaimed, unloved, a waste of a life . . .

Truck driver Robert Eden did not hesitate to stop when he was flagged down by housewife Maybel Harrison on the northbound section of Highway 89, just half a mile north of Squaw Valley Creek, on the edge of those same High Sierras, near Tahoe City, in Placer County, California. It was dawn on July 17, 1984.

"There's a brushfire by the creek," explained Maybel breathlessly.

Eden grabbed the chemical fire extinguisher from the cab of his truck and ran to the blaze just thirty yards from the side of the road. Minutes later he also doused the still burning fire with a three gallon can of water, just to be absolutely certain it was completely out. Then he found himself transfixed by what Maybel Harrison thought was a mannequin—the toes sticking out from under the cinders confirmed it.

"That's a body. . . ."

The silver duct tape used to gag the victim and tie her wrists was still visible on the charred remains.

Just over an hour later, with emergency services surrounding the scene, Tahoe City Fire Department Captain Ron Collins—a member of the Arson Task Force—began examining the rubble with a hydrocarbon detector, which determines the presence of flammable liquids in fires. It took less than a minute to establish that the fire had been started deliberately.

Tahoe City Detective Russell Potts then carefully collected three soil samples starting at a point four feet north of the corpse. Then he crouched down to collect more soil just six inches from the charred remains before removing one last sample from a different angle to the body. They were all carefully packaged in contamination-free cans, sealed and put aside for eventual analysis by the Department of Justice.

By 7:50 A.M. detectives had already informed the Department of Justice that they were dealing with a homicide and requested that a photographer and criminologist get to the site immediately.

At 10:05 A.M., Placer County Sheriff Donald J. Nunes arrived with a police photographer. Within the hour, criminologist Michael Saggs from the Department of Justice and four officials were snapping away furiously with their cameras at the grotesquely twisted body that consisted of a charred left arm propped up on her elbow, with the hand straight up in a curled position. The lower portion of the left leg was detached at the femur and was lying on the ground approximately three inches away from the end of the femur. The right arm was at the corpse's side and the right leg extended straight from the body at a weird right angle.

Investigators did not allow Mark Dafforn from the discreetly named "county removal service" to take control of the body until 2:00 P.M. Detectives frequently find homicide scenes tampered with before they even arrive at a location. But on this occasion, they actually had the luxury of more than eight hours of light to minutely examine the area for clues. Police sifted through a vast array of belongings found near or on the body, including perfume, writing paper, necklaces, bracelets, clothing, a toothbrush, even a fork and soup spoon. But there was no actual evidence of the victim's identity.

Detectives decided it was time to rechristen the charred remains as Jane Doe #4873/84.

That day, an urgent telecommunication was faxed to the U.S. Missing Persons Bureau.

It read:

WEA 18–22 YRS. BLN HAIR, SLENDER BUILD, POSS WEARING A YELLOW NYLON HOODED PARKA AND UN-KNOWN COLOR CORDUROY PANTS.

THIS DEPARTMENT IS CURRENTLY INVESTIGATING A HOMICIDE WHICH HAS OCCURRED IN OUR COUNTY AT APPROXIMATELY 0545 HRS THIS DATE. VICTIM WAS FOUND BY A PASSING MOTORIST. VICTIM HAD SILVER DUCT TAPE COVERING HER MOUTH, AND AROUND BOTH WRISTS. VICTIM WAS THEN SET ON FIRE AT THE SIDE OF THE ROAD. VICTIM WAS VERY BADLY BURNED, AND UN-RECOGNIZABLE. VICTIM HAD SOME PERSONAL PROPERTY WITH HER, POSS IN 2 PLASTIC GARBAGE BAGS. BAGS CON-TAINED MISC PERSONAL PROPERTY, INCLUDING CHIL-DRENS CLOTHING, HOWEVER BAGS WERE ALSO BURNED.

REQUEST YOU CHECK YOUR RECORDS FOR ANY MISS-ING PERSONS WHICH MAY MATCH THIS JANE DOE, OR ANY SIMILAR HOMICIDES.

THANKS IN ADVANCE.

REFER: LT CADER/DET LIDDLE CASE #4858–84
PLACER COUNTY SHERIFF'S SUBSTATION, DRAWER

1710, TAHOE CITY, CA. 95730 DONALD P. NUNES SHER-
IFF/CORONER (916) 583-1561 7/17/84

1358 HRS NTS/PJO

The day after the discovery of the corpse, detectives
sent the victim's fingers off to Sacramento to have
prints taken off them after police began to suspect that
the body might have been that of a missing woman
called Georgia Darlene Taylor. The practice of removing fingers from a corpse is a little known procedure
which is rarely referred to because it is considered by
some to be a disrespectful way to treat a body. But investigators across the world have been using this
method of checking fingerprints for years, because it
saves having to move entire corpses across state lines
and in some cases international borders. Recently, a
Florida medical examiner was transporting a victim's
fingers across the state when he was stopped by the
Florida Highway Patrol for allegedly speeding. When
the official explained to the motorbike cop what he had
in the box on the seat next to him, the officer refused to
believe him and forced him to open the container. The
policeman fainted on the spot.

Back in Sacramento, an examination of the prints on
the duct tape found wrapped around part of the body
confirmed that two men implicated in the Georgia
Darlene Taylor case were not involved in the death of
this particular Jane Doe. To add to their frustration,
investigators could find no match for the prints on the
state computer file.

The subsequent autopsy—performed by forensic scientist Dr. A. V. Cunha at the DeWitt Center Morgue on July 23—provided the police with few clues to Jane Doe's killer. All they could be certain of was that she was five feet three inches, weighed approximately 115 to 130 pounds, and had blond hair and blue eyes. However, the examination did uncover that she had died *after* being bound, gagged, and set on fire. Dr. Cunha also found a large ovarian tumor in the corpse, which indicated she had been severely beaten in the stomach.

Dr. Cunha was also puzzled by the apparent presence of two recent wounds in the right back and lower buttocks region. But the corpse was too badly charred for him to recognize the exact causes of each injury.

However, the one aspect of the discovery of the body that had investigators instantly very concerned were the diapers found near the body, plus what they thought were children's clothing. Detectives feared that this Jane Doe might have been with a child who could have been killed elsewhere. Only later did they acknowledge that the "children's clothing" were actually just skimpy teenagers' blouses.

The final pathological diagnoses by Dr. Cunha referred to *ninety percent* burns to the body and described those previously inflicted wounds as being of "uncertain significance."

Dental examiner James Nordstrom was able to be more helpful. He reported that the victim had a chipped tooth, possibly caused during an attack, and a number of fillings that might make identification easier.

However, a computer check could not match up those dental records, and Placer County detectives believed it was unlikely they would establish identity of the corpse, let alone solve the case. Putting a name and family to a murder victim is usually the most significant development in trying to investigate a homicide. Without a name, there is basically no one to interview, unless of course there were some witnesses.

So it was that just eight days later, Sheriff Donald Nunes made a formal request to have the body of their Jane Doe #4873/84 frozen at the Sacramento County Coroner's Office until further inquiries could be made. Publicly, police were continuing their investigation as energetically as ever. Privately, they were winding down the entire probe because they had reached a complete and utter dead end. By freezing her body in case it should be needed for evidence/identity purposes at a later date, the sheriff was simply going through the motions just in case a miracle occurred and they got a break on the case.

Jane Doe's face was even reconstructed by police artist Jim Hahn on the day before her remains were taken off to be frozen in Sacramento. Detectives hoped that the drawing might provoke some response once they printed up posters, but they did not hold out much hope.

On August 1, 1984, Placer County investigators tried one last telecommunication message, this time to narcotics units, vice units, biker units, intelligence units, and sex crime units nationwide in a final effort to identify their Jane Doe. They got no response.

At the end of August a continuation report filed by Placer County Sheriff's Department was sent to Sheriff Nunes informing him that more than two hundred possible leads had been investigated into the identity of the corpse. The report concluded that their biggest hope was that when schools reopened in the later part of September, they might get a reaction to those posters distributed to every school district in the state.

When fall came and that drew a complete blank, the Sheriff's Department—rather than incur any more expensive freezer charges at the Sacramento Medical Examiner's Office—released the body for burial at the New Auburn District Cemetery in Auburn. The funeral was unattended. No one ever knew her real name.

The following spring, the FBI contacted the Placer County Sheriff's Department in Auburn, with 235 possible matches for the Jane Doe. But they soon proved negative.

The main problem for police was that unsolved murders in the rural Sierra counties divided by major highways were a logistical nightmare. Virtually all the homicides were imported; in other words, they happened elsewhere and then became their case because the bodies were dumped on their turf.

Most cases tended to be shifted quietly to the back of homicide files. Detectives prepared to wait for a lead that, in most cases, never surfaced. The mystery of Jane Doe #4873/84 would remain unsolved for almost ten years.

Almost one year later, on June 21, 1985, a fisherman discovered a corpse in a box on the edge of Martis Creek Lake, located just east of Highway 267 in the densely forested Martis Valley area of Nevada County, California, just fifteen miles from where that other body had been dumped and set on fire. He immediately alerted Elmer Barber, camp host at the Martis Creek Lake Campground, to the existence of the corpse. Barber went straight to the local sheriff's office where he told Deputy Gary Costley all about the "body in the box."

At 12:40 P.M. Officer Costley drove up the paved road, past the Tahoe Truckee Sanitation Agency building, turned east and then followed the road as it swept to the north and headed onto another paved road clearly marked with a campground sign. Just past the campground, the road turned to gravel and dirt before sweeping to the left and straightening out once more at the location by the lake where Elmer Barber said the body had been found. Deputy Costley found the box—measuring just twenty-five inches by nineteen inches—in amongst a clump of young weeping willows, which covered an area of only about twelve feet by eight feet near the water's edge.

Costley tentatively pulled open the top of the box—clearly marked "Popcorn Cups"—to examine the contents. Inside were stained sheets, blankets, and plastic bags. On closer inspection, Costley could clearly see a left arm and shoulder, the left side of a torso, and the left hips of a human body in a fetal position. The body ranged in color from a light, almost white color, to green, purple, and black. There was also a cloth ligature around the deceased's neck and wrist.

Tire tracks near the scene were evident, but because of rain that morning they were not clear enough to be identified.

At 2:00 P.M. six more policemen arrived on the scene followed by Deputy D.A. Tom Eckhardt. The officials had another problem on their hands besides the homicide: Whose jurisdiction covered the crime scene—Placer or Nevada County? On the basis of the corpse being discovered a few feet inside their county line, Nevada took on the investigation.

By the time the body was removed a few hours later by Medical Examiner's official Joe Aguera and taken to the Tahoe-Truckee Mortuary for an autopsy the next day, police had combed the area but failed to find any other clues apart from the box. Its grotesque contents also included a discarded pair of white panties and a pair of dirty white socks. Investigators noted that the Jane Doe had three pierced right ears and two pierced left.

The Nevada County Coroner's Record form filled in that day had few actual facts recorded, just more than a dozen "unknowns" written in the information boxes. The coroner had been unable to determine whether the victim had starved or suffocated in that box. Another Jane Doe was about to be christened after death.

It would take almost ten years before the tragic lives of those two seemingly unconnected corpses would be linked to reveal a horrific story that stunned law officers in two states.

One

Hell hath no fury like a woman
scorned . . .

Theresa Jimmie Sanders's facial structure might not have been particularly classic, and the perpetual frown she wore gave her blue pupils more of a haunted look than the clear-eyed confidence that she wished they'd had, but eighteen-year-old Theresa was still brunette and pretty, if not beautiful. Her complexion was clear and smooth, and her five-foot-five-inch frame was lithe and bosomy.

Resident Sheriff's Deputy Fred May had vaguely noticed Theresa a few weeks earlier when she and her husband moved into one of the row of small, single-story houses just near the railroad tracks about fifty yards down from his own home on Elm Avenue in Galt, a township twelve miles south of Sacramento, California. He therefore instantly recognized the striking-looking teenage mother when she turned up on his doorstep at 9:15 A.M. on July 6, 1964.

"You gotta come quick. I shot my husband in the arm."

Within a few minutes, Galt Police Chief Walter

11

Froehlich was also on the scene and the two men accompanied the young girl—with her baby in her arms—to her home at 586 Elm, where they found her husband Clifford lying facedown in the doorway of the kitchen. His only wound appeared at first to be in the wrist. But the .30-30 caliber slug had traveled through his body and embedded itself in his heart. He was dead.

The two officers immediately glanced at an old model deer rifle leaning against a wall in the front room. Noticing their interest, Theresa told the chief: "I grabbed the gun to make him keep from hitting me and it went off."

She told them a tearful story about how her husband had begun to thrash her with the butt end of the rifle and how, miraculously, she had been able to wrestle the weapon away from him. She even said to the policemen that Clifford Sanders had been arrested just two weeks earlier for assault and battery, but she had decided not to press charges.

"Her reaction was mild, I'd say," recalled Froehlich almost thirty years later. "But different people react in different ways."

Theresa Sanders was booked and taken to the Sacramento County Jail. Her baby son Howard—still ten days off celebrating his first birthday—was taken by the sheriff to one of Theresa's relatives north of Sacramento.

The day after the shooting, the *Sacramento Bee* daily newspaper ran a dramatic photo of pretty, petite Theresa Sanders being led into the county jail by stern-looking Galt Police Matron Mary Templeton, a whole head and shoulders taller than her prisoner. Arms folded, her hair cut in a fashionable bob style, Theresa Sanders looked as if butter would not melt in her mouth.

The headline that accompanied the photo exclaimed: MURDER CHARGE IS DUE IN GALT DEATH.

Its first attention-grabbing paragraph read:

> Deputy District Attorney Donald Dorfman said he planned to file a murder charge today against eighteen-year-old Mrs. Theresa Sanders of Galt in the deer rifle slaying of her husband. Clifford Sanders, 23, was slain yesterday morning in the couple's small Galt home. Investigators reported the .30-30 bullet apparently grazed off his left wrist and lodged in his heart . . .

The shooting was the talk of Galt—a sleepy railroad town split in two by the old Highway 99 that runs up from Stockton and Modesto to Sacramento. The Sanders had moved to their tiny, one-bedroom house from Sacramento earlier that summer. Conditions inside the house were especially cramped because of the presence of Theresa's father, James Cross. There was no actual bath or shower in the $75-a-month property, and baby Howard was usually bathed by Theresa in the kitchen sink. The difficult conditions were not helped by the roar of endless cargo trains regularly thundering along the railroad, just a few yards from their front door.

The red-roofed, white building they lived in was really no bigger than a single garage, and contrasted drastically with the larger, more luxurious three- and four-bedroom homes on Elm, just fifty yards in the opposite direction to the railroad tracks. Up until the shooting, Theresa, Clifford, and Howard slept in a small room at the back of the house, while her father James slept on a couch in the living room, just by the rickety front door.

After her arrest, Theresa Sanders told Deputy District Attorney Donald Dorfman that her husband had threatened to beat her on the morning of the shooting and that he was packing to leave her. But she also admitted that he had not actually beaten her since the incident that almost led to him being arrested two weeks earlier.

It then transpired that just minutes before the killing, Theresa Sanders went into the bedroom where the rifle was kept loaded, got the gun, and returned to the living room as her husband was about to open the door, apparently to leave home for good.

"I remember holding the gun and having my finger on the trigger, but then everything went blank," she told investigators at the time.

Theresa Sanders's invalid father, James Cross, informed detectives that the gun was kept loaded with the safety catch on. Significantly, he also added that it would have been necessary for her to deliberately cock the hammer before firing it.

The couple had been estranged at the time, but Clifford Sanders—a carpenter for the American Safeway Scaffolding Company—had moved back into the Galt home with his wife and father-in-law about three weeks before the shooting.

The only witness to the killing was the couple's eleven-month-old baby, Howard. He said later he was haunted by the knowledge that he was there when his mother shot his father dead, even though he was too young to actually remember the killing.

Within a few hours of Theresa Sanders's arrest for murder, she told investigators she was pregnant with another child by her late husband. That unborn child was Sheila, a girl whose future was to be irretrievably connected to that fatal shooting.

On August 4, 1964, Theresa Sanders entered a plea of innocent by reason of self-defense in a Sacramento court to the charge of murdering her husband. She insisted she only intended to scare Clifford Sanders when the rifle she was holding went off, sending that bullet into his heart.

Her performance at the trial was considered very emotive by attorneys and police alike. She even tearfully told her own lawyer: "All I want to do is to go home and take care of my baby."

Deputy District Attorney Donald Dorfman was not so convinced. He argued for a first degree murder conviction and insisted that Theresa Sanders was jealous of her husband's attentions to other women and had regularly threatened to kill him.

"Not every murderer looks like the witch in *Snow White*," he told the jury.

Theresa Sanders looked a lot less like the witch than she did Snow White: pure, sensible, sweet.

Dorfman insisted that just after the shooting, Theresa Sanders ran across the street and told a neighbor she had just shot her husband. Then, her cheeks burning and her pretty face twisted into a scowl, she added: "No man's going to leave me."

When Dorfman tried to introduce that evidence in court, the judge ruled it as inadmissible because the neighbor was the wife of the deputy sheriff and Theresa should have been advised of her rights.

Two extra bailiffs were even assigned to the trial after Theresa's husband's brother, Tommy Sanders, said he was "going to get a gun and shoot someone." A witness at the trial, Tommy openly displayed his anger toward Theresa.

At one stage, the judge even permitted Theresa Sanders's attorney, Robert A. Zarick, to carry a loaded handgun to court.

Once, he took the gun out of his briefcase, turned to the victim's family, seated in the courtroom, and said: "None of you maniacs are going to get me like Cliff tried to get her." It was a trial filled with controversy.

Theresa Sanders's pitiful story of life at the hands of a wife beater who also frequently boasted of his prowess with other women, was totally contradicted by her husband's sister Mrs. Lydia Hansen. She told the court that her brother worked hard, never drank, and gave his wife all his earnings. These claims have a familiar ring to them, as Theresa's children later complained bitterly about how their mother made them hand over all their earnings every week.

Hansen, Theresa's sister-in-law at the time, also insisted that her brother never once threatened or hit his pretty young wife. In fact, Hansen recalled that Theresa always drove her husband to work and back to be sure no other women ever got to look at him. She also kept his clothes in rags for the same reason, and gave Clifford Sanders just fifty cents for lunch money so he could not go to a restaurant where another woman might get a look at him.

Hansen also revealed that Theresa Sanders had shot at her husband once before, and that her brother had shown her the bullet hole in the floor.

"I believe with all my heart that Theresa Sanders planned to kill my brother," she insisted to the hushed courtroom.

But then, in a remarkable show of compassion, Hansen said she wanted Sanders to go free so she could raise her brother's children. Hansen's final statement may have done more than anything else to sway the jury, and that decision could well have contributed toward the tragedies that later occurred in Theresa's household.

On September 10—just twelve days after the trial began—a jury of nine men and three women told Judge Charles W. Johnson that they found Theresa Sanders not guilty as charged, after deliberating for an hour and forty-five minutes.

Theresa, dressed in a baby-blue maternity dress on that last day in court, wept when the verdict was announced. Then she approached the jury box. Many of the jurors smiled at her. She was desperately trying to thank them, but the tears just would not stop streaming down her face.

One female juror grinned warmly at Theresa Sanders and got up to put her arm around the innocent young mother. It was a touching scene.

Theresa Sanders held her weak little chin high and pursed her thin lips together in triumph.

Former chief Froehlich, now a crusty seventy-five-year-old, believes to this day that District Attorney Dorfman thought he had a clear-cut case against her.

Dorfman had tried to give the court the impression that Theresa Sanders was a cold, calculating killer. A few days later—in yet another strange twist in the even stranger life of this alleged murderess—Theresa coolly walked into Dorfman's office to reclaim the rifle she had used to kill her husband.

She even told Dorfman: "I liked the way you came after me."

Theresa Sanders was oddly in awe of the young prosecutor, and years later she even tried to hire him to handle the divorce proceedings for her third marriage. She also recommended Dorfman to that same tragic child, Howard, when his own marriage began to crumble more than twenty years later.

Theresa told her family that Dorfman was a superb attorney and she had great respect for him.

But Chief Froehlich's most vivid memory of the aftermath following Theresa Sanders's arrest was that of little Howard Sanders. Froehlich personally drove the child to a suburb north of Sacramento to stay with relatives while Theresa was in custody.

"That poor little fella. I always wondered what happened to him."

Thirty years later, Howard Sanders has just one reminder of his father still in his possession. It is a rusted handgun with a broken handle.

Theresa Sanders could not stand the thought of moving back into the house where she shot her husband dead, so she, her father, and her baby Howard moved to the district of Rio Linda, North Sacramento, after her acquittal on murder charges. It was familiar territory for Theresa, since she had been born in Rio Linda on March 14, 1946.

Little is known about her true upbringing, apart from the fact that her mother died in her arms when Theresa was about twelve. Her father had a close bond with his daughter and remained a part of her life right up until his death in 1985. But Theresa Sanders spun such a vast web of lies to so many different people that much of what she told about her past has to now be completely discounted.

She told some friends about pleasant countryside, life on a farm, and riding horses every day. But to others, she reshaped her past to include an unhappy childhood, poverty-line existence, and a daily regime of brutality at the hands of a series of stepmothers. The truth is that no one really knows much about Theresa's life before she was arrested for murdering Clifford Sanders in July 1964.

By Christmas of that year, Theresa Sanders had put her brush with the law behind her. Already in the later stages of her second pregnancy, she went back to calling herself by her maiden name, Theresa Cross, and settled back into life in a modest two-bedroom house at 6608 Cherry Lane, Rio Linda.

At twenty-two minutes past midnight on March 13, 1965—the day before her own birthday—Theresa, still just eighteen, gave birth to Sheila Gay Sanders, at the Roseville District Hospital, just a few miles from her home. On Sheila's birth certificate Theresa had written *Deceased* under the sections marked "Husband's Present or Last Occupation" and "Kind of Industry or Business."

By the end of the following year, Theresa revived her interest in men and met handsome young marine Robert Wallace Knorr. She had also moved to a comfortable house on Tioga Street, in San Francisco. Life seemed to be looking up.

Theresa gave birth to her third child, Suesan Marline Knorr, at 1:50 A.M. on September 27, 1966, at the USAF Hospital on Mather Air Force Base, in central California. The birth certainly caused a stir among Robert Knorr's family back in Minnesota. After all, he was only eighteen and the mother of his child was just twenty—and they had not even bothered to get married.

However, Knorr family pressure eventually resulted in Robert and Theresa going through a wedding ceremony in 1966. On September 15, 1967, a son, William Robert, was born. On December 31 the following year came Robert Wallace Jr. Theresa Knorr was just twenty-two years old and the mother of five young children.

Theresa Knorr and the children found themselves on the receiving end of some attacks by her husband in the years following the birth of their children. According to her son, Howard, Robert Knorr's temper, combined with his experiences in Vietnam, had turned him into a highly volatile character. The children came to fear his presence in the house. One time, Howard had to pick his baby brother Billy Bob off the floor when Knorr Sr. kicked his son all the way across the room into a toilet and his head split open.

Theresa Knorr all too frequently became the last line of defense against her ill-tempered husband.

By the time a sixth child, Theresa (Terry), was born on August 5, 1970, at the Sutter Memorial Hospital, Theresa Knorr had already separated from her husband Robert. At the end of September that year, their divorce was finalized.

Two marriages followed in fast succession for Theresa Knorr. First there was Ronald Pulliam. Of all her husbands, he seems to be the only one no one has a bad thing to say about. The children even called him "Dad" when they all lived together in a comfortable house on Morris Avenue, in Sacramento, although the entire family lost touch with him years ago.

In February 1994, Pulliam said he just wanted to forget he had ever had a relationship with Theresa Knorr, let alone a marriage.

"I don't want to talk about her. It all happened a long time ago," were the only words he would utter.

Pulliam and Theresa broke up in the early seventies. A man called Bill Bullington then came on the scene, but none of the surviving children ever knew if their mother actually married him.

By 1973 the family had moved into their one and only large home—in Orangevale, West Sacramento. It was to be their home for longer than all their other places put together, and actually had enough space for the entire clan. Theresa then met and married a wealthy newspaper executive called Chester Harris, who worked on the now defunct *Sacramento Union*.

Around this time, Theresa Knorr began putting on weight. She also started to grow her long dark hair farther down her back, giving her the appearance of some kind of medieval witch. Chet Harris had an interest in the occult, and he soon found a keen disciple in Theresa.

Two

Abusive parents thrive on isolation and
a perverted sense of privacy.
Paul Mones, *When a Child Kills*

There is no evidence of the much stressed, over-worked, Theresa Knorr hitting out impatiently at her children when they were toddlers. She actually enjoyed bringing up the youngsters in those early years. She saw herself as the all-powerful mom who would ensure her children's survival through thick and thin.

Theresa Knorr often took youngest daughter, Terry, and her brother Robert to the local Dairy Queen for a slap-up lunch followed by a big dollop of ice cream, and made them both promise not to tell their older brothers and sisters, who were at school, and would no doubt be jealous that they had not been taken out for a treat.

Theresa Knorr also made many other sacrifices on behalf of the children. One time, she even pawned her favorite diamond bracelet so that she could buy Terry some school clothes.

She was the only person the children knew as consistently loving them and taking care of them. She was their life. Their savior.

Throughout this period, Robert Knorr Sr. was like a

black cloud looming over the Knorr household. He still came to visit his four children just about whenever he felt like it, and sometimes ended up kicking the hell out of the kids if the mood suited him. His temper got even more frayed when he suffered a serious shrapnel wound in the stomach in Vietnam. He also walked with a slight limp.

Theresa Knorr's weight was still rising rapidly and she had taken up reading the Bible at every opportunity. She would sit in the living room and recite from the Bible, often underlining quotations and sometimes even forcing the children to join in as well.

But in another corner of that large house in Orangevale, a much more disturbing incident was occurring.

Terry, just six years old, was being molested by her brother Howard, who was thirteen at the time. It was an awful introduction to an even more awful life within those four brutal walls.

Terry explained to investigators more than fifteen years later: "I didn't know what he was doing; well, I knew what he was doing wasn't right, but I wasn't, you know, I was afraid to tell anybody, and . . . I went to my mom because it hurt."

Theresa Knorr was outraged when she heard that Howard had molested his half sister. She broke a chair over the boy's back and seriously beat him to make sure he never did it again.

Howard Sanders later confessed to having illicit sex with his sister in dramatic tones to two stunned Placer County investigators during a tape-recorded interview conducted at his home in Sacramento on November 16, 1993.

POLICE OFFICER: I'm going to make this very short and sweet. There's been allegations of molestation and that you molested Theresa, your sister. Are those allegations true?

SANDERS: Yes.

POLICE OFFICER: And that was sodomy, anal sex.

SANDERS: Yes.

Terry will never know if that attack by her brother sparked the eventual terrors that filled the Knorr household, but shortly after being molested by Howard, bad things started to happen.

The first incident occurred when the mother of one of Terry's best friends, Jennifer—who lived on Sutton, just around the corner from the house in Orangevale—called at Theresa Knorr's front door to offer her some of her daughter's clothes as a gift.

Theresa Knorr was furious. She thought Terry was going around telling people that the family didn't have any money, that they were so poor they couldn't afford to buy the children clothes.

Once Jennifer's mother had gone, as later recounted by Terry, Theresa Knorr grabbed her youngest daughter and made her strip naked before dragging her through the house.

Then she grabbed a piece of rope, wrapped it around Terry's neck and threw it over a door. Theresa Knorr's two sons, Billy Bob and Robert, then held the rope, forcing Terry to stay in one position while her mother beat her with a weeping willow limb until she almost passed out. Terry remained jammed against the door throughout.

Theresa Knorr's violent outbursts seemed to escalate when she was introduced to witchcraft by Chester Harris after he became her husband.

Theresa immediately began claiming that her daughter Suesan was involved in devil worshiping. And she began making veiled references to Suesan plotting to kill her mother before she reached the age of eighteen.

"To fulfill her contract with the devil . . ."

According to Terry, something happened between Chester Harris and Suesan. It was something that may have driven a wedge between her and her mother. It also had the effect of breaking up Theresa Knorr's marriage to Harris.

After the split with Harris, Theresa Knorr began frequently disappearing from the house on Bellingham, in Orangevale, for days at a time, leaving Howard—just fourteen—to look after the rest of the clan.

On one occasion she took off for at least four days after running out of the door of the house in front of the children. She came back with the police, claiming that Howard had threatened her.

Howard—sitting in the living room with a friend—cried because he felt so betrayed by his mother's abandonment and her false accusations against him.

Years later Howard wondered whether Theresa Knorr had been suffering from a nervous breakdown at the time. What other reason could there be for a mother to run out the front door and leave her children in the care of a fourteen-year-old?

Theresa Knorr gave her son a bizarre explanation when he asked where she had been during those four days she disappeared.

"She told me she had found some pennies and she threw these pennies away and that, you know, these pennies showed back up in the motel where she was staying, and no matter what she did, these pennies kept showing back up, you know," said Howard.

"I mean, I didn't understand it at the time. But looking back on it, I mean, obviously they were paranoid delusions. And that goes along with somebody that's having a nervous breakdown."

Sometime after this, Theresa Knorr stopped getting out of bed and getting dressed. She never took a shower, and refused to go outside for weeks at a time. But she still managed to wield the hand of discipline if required.

Theresa Knorr stopped punishing her son Howard when he was a strapping fourteen-year-old—six feet and 190 pounds—and highly likely to retaliate against his overweight, overbearing mom. The last time he was beaten by her, she wielded her favorite weapon—a two-by-four with the words "Board of Education" written across it.* He cannot remember the reasons for the punishment, but the words exchanged between mother and son provide a cold insight into their relationship.

* Henry Lee Lucas, one of the most notorious serial killers of modern times, was beaten regularly by his mother with a two-by-four at his home in Blacksburg, Virginia. He went on to receive eleven murder convictions, including a death penalty, six life sentences, two seventy-five-year sentences, and one sixty-year sentence. He is currently on death row in Huntsville, Texas.

After his mother's final painful smack on his backside with the two-by-four, Howard turned around to her and said:

"You done now?"

"Yes. I guess you're too big to whip anymore."

Howard's worst legacy from those beatings was his vicious temper. Life at that house really screwed him up.

"I had a real problem with my anger, you know, real problem with my anger. That's what led me into a bad marriage, and I ended up going to jail for it and that wasn't the first time I ever got in trouble about violence. So yeah, it screwed me up pretty good. I had a lot of demons to work out," he told investigators years later.

But while Theresa Knorr might have decided not to beat her eldest son anymore, there was no such reprieve for her daughters.

She was convinced they were going to go out and be promiscuous. She wanted to keep control of the girls so they would never be involved with boys. That meant clamping down on them—not even letting them go out and socialize with other teenagers.

Theresa also passed on the mantle of responsibility to her boys, especially Howard at that time, because he was the eldest. It put the teenager under immense pressure. He was already working part-time as a cook at a local restaurant called Joe and Dotty's, on Auburn Boulevard, to help the family survive. He had learned how to cook by preparing meals for his brothers and sisters. But now he was going to have to be the father as well.

The other children accepted Howard as a father figure for the period he remained at home. He was respected, even feared. Basically, he took the place of a husband. That also meant frequently being the disciplinarian of the family.

There were numerous occasions when Theresa Knorr would let Howard do her spanking for her with that familiar piece of two-by-four. She was proud of having trained him in the art of inflicting punishment.

Sometimes Howard would make the children hold their ankles as he smashed the board on their bottoms or lay them on the floor before spanking them.

These spankings were such vicious beatings that none of the children ever forgot them.

Bruises were commonplace, especially when Howard used that two-by-four piece of wood—the Board of Education.

Theresa Knorr still got involved in the really serious punishments. On many occasions the children being punished would end up with bruises all over their bodies.

Theresa Knorr even introduced a switch-style riding crop just to inflict extra pain on her flock of children.

When she used the switch, the injuries were so serious that the other children would dab peroxide on the cuts all over the back of whoever had been punished.

As the oldest and the biggest, no one dared argue with Howard. He even devised rules and regulations that the other children had to obey, or face dire consequences.

Howard's career as main male enforcer in the Knorr household continued until he retired, at sixteen, after starting to work full-time as a chef. Howard was the sort of guy who, if the front door was slammed, went around to the back door; and if the back door was locked, he tried the windows; and if the windows were barred, he would haul out a sledgehammer.

But working outside the home began to give him a new perspective on life.

"I was seeing more of life and started to realize that these weren't right, you know, that beating kids wasn't right," he says.

As well as questioning his mother's orders, Howard actually began standing up against Theresa Knorr on behalf of his other brothers and sisters. The punisher was transforming into the protector.

She was no longer physically strong enough to stand up against Howard, but she had no intention of stopping the punishments being inflicted. She just tried to make sure he wasn't around when she handed out her own special brand of discipline.

Howard never actually hit his mother, but he did come close to it frequently. One time he grabbed her and threw her against a wall. Then he smashed the wall right next to her head with his fist and put a hole in it. The children used to snigger every time they walked past the dent in the plaster.

But it was sisters Suesan and Sheila who got the brunt of their mother's vicious temper. Howard and Terry both remember one day when Theresa Knorr pulled Sheila's canine tooth out with her bare hands because it was not growing straight.

At school Sheila's big ears earned her the nickname Dumbo. Life was extra tough on her. Physical abuse at home and verbal taunting at school. Was there no escape?

Theresa Knorr's drinking also got so excessive at this time that she frequently would pack all six children in the family station wagon and leave them in the car outside bars she liked to frequent in Orangevale. Visits to drive-in movies were just as distressful for the youngsters.

"She'd end up getting bombed. She'd pass out and we'd have to wait for her to wake up to go home," recalled Howard.

For many of their childhood years the kids veered from malnourishment to being force-fed vast quantities of fatty food. Sometimes teachers would take pity on some of the Knorr children and provide them with sandwiches and the occasional hot meal. But it is tragically clear the diet inside that household had serious effects. By the time he was twelve, Howard's diet included a daily consumption of alcohol and drugs, packs of cigarettes, and the occasional slice of bread smothered in peanut butter, jelly, or cheese. These years of inconsistent, damaging diet, especially during childhood, may well have resulted in stunted development of some of the Knorr children. It also created levels of stress and fear that no ordinary family should ever have to suffer. But there was much worse to come . . .

Three

If my mother loved you, she loved you
greatly. But if you were on the outs
with my mother, she would make you
feel like you were all alone in the
universe, that nobody cared about you
and you weren't worth anything. So you
always wanted to be on the good side
of my mother.
Howard Sanders

That's odd, neighbor Sean Martin remembered thinking as he walked out into the backyard of his house opposite the Knorr family home in Orangevale, the dog is not moving.

Bijou just lay there deathly still as twelve-year-old Sean tried desperately to wake him up. He pulled and tugged at the animal, but there were no signs of life in his tiny body.

A few minutes later Sean Martin and his big brother Chris started flashing a light down the dog's throat. They just could not accept that their pet—part cocker spaniel, part poodle—was dead. When it dawned on them what had actually happened, both boys began to cry.

Life on Bellingham Way had been littered with odd incidents ever since the Knorrs moved in nine years earlier. Those who visited the house likened it to an out of control runaway train ride consisting of drug taking, excessive alcohol, and repeated violence toward one or another of the Knorr children. The family got a reputation in the area, which meant they were blamed for just about every strange occurrence on the street.

To make matters worse, Howard Sanders had reached his mid-teens and was hanging out with all the wrong types.

Neighbor Sean Martin grew up with the entire Knorr family from the mid-seventies up until when Theresa Knorr sold the house in 1982. He witnessed dozens of odd incidents, but the death of his dog Bijou is a typical example of how rumors could quickly spread about the "weird" Knorr family.

It all began when Bijou nipped youngest daughter Terry on her leg one time when she was teasing him in the front yard of Sean's home. Terry—eleven at the time—was not that bothered about the injury, but Theresa Knorr was convinced the dog had rabies, and she reported Sean and his family to the SPCA and got the dog quarantined for a month.

Bijou was actually released from quarantine after only four days because he was given a complete clean bill of health. The next day Sean walked into the backyard and found the animal dead.

No one knows who killed the dog, but Sean believes it was poisoned. The incident went down in Bellingham folklore as gossip flew around that Theresa Knorr had killed the dog. But no one ever proved if the story was true.

The Knorr house in Orangevale had a strangely designed interior. The orange and white drapes were thumbtacked to the wall, and there were just bare lightbulbs—no lamp shades.

The furnishing inside the house consisted of a very basic leaf table with six chairs around it. One tatty couch. But there were no knickknacks or posters or pictures on the walls, and the TV was on constantly. The carpet was a dreadful, sickly, pea-green color. It seemed as if personal touches were nonexistent inside the Knorr family home.

Sean Martin—now twenty-four, and working as a doorman at one of Sacramento's biggest sports bars by night while going to school during the day—got into trouble with Robert one time when they were just twelve years old. The two boys stole hundreds of dimes out of a neighbor's house.

After being caught, both boys accused each other of committing the evil deed. Sean's mother marched him down to her neighbor's house to apologize for stealing. Then she took him to the Knorrs.

On their arrival at the house, the front door opened and there was a stench of marijuana wafting onto the porch. One of the Knorr children hollered for their mother, but was ordered to slam the door shut, and Sean's mother never did actually get to talk to Theresa Knorr about their respective sons' illicit behavior.

Sean frequently heard screaming and pounding on the walls while playing on the sidewalk near the house. But instead of reporting the noises, he just tried to avoid going near the house. Other neighbors commented on the noises, but they also did nothing.

On other occasions, Sean heard streams of profanities coming from Theresa Knorr inside the house. It surprised him that an avid Bible reader should use such foul language.

Sean only ever got to talk to Theresa Knorr during her rare trips out to the local store when she would walk past his front yard. The conversation was always brief and ineffectual. Theresa Knorr—whose weight had soared beyond the 200-pound mark by this time— would waddle up the street with her long dark hair down to her waist and wearing a vast pair of bell-bottom pants. She looked like a huge, fat version of the lady out of the Addams Family, he remembered years later.

Sean also suspected some sort of devil worshiping going on inside the Knorr house. It coincided with the time the children were made to shave their heads by their mother and wear certain types of clothes. But once again, no one did anything to bring the family to the attention of the authorities.

Not surprisingly, the Knorr children never wanted to go home when they were out playing with their friends.

Terry and Billy Bob were constantly around Sean's home, which had become known locally as the "Kool-Aid house" because it was such a relaxed place. The Knorr children stayed there for meals and told their friends they rarely got a proper meal at home. Other neighbors also felt sorry for them and would feed them regularly.

Older sister Sheila was frequently dispatched by Theresa Knorr to pick up the children from neighbors' homes. She was always very well-mannered and would turn up at the door and say: "Okay kids, time to come home."

Sean was in the same class at school as Robert for four years, but during that time the youngster was often absent. Robert also surprised his friend Sean by regularly referring to his mother in a detrimental fashion.

"He said she was off her rocker. That she was a hermit with emotional problems. He just kept saying she was crazy," recalled Sean.

One time, Theresa Knorr set fire to the backyard of the house on Bellingham for no apparent reason. When Sean rushed over to see if he could help, he had to go through the garage to the back yard, and noticed hundreds of articles of clothing just ripped to shreds, lining the concrete floor. The fire destroyed the back fence, but Sean never forgot the sight of all those clothes. No one ever did find out why the fire occurred.

All the Knorr children—except for Howard Sanders —were very skinny and undernourished-looking at this time. Neighbor Sean also noticed welts on Robert's back from where his mom had beaten him with a belt.

Sean and Robert regularly did drugs together. Sometimes they would sneak out and smoke pot in the nearby park. Later, they did some more serious stuff together.

Some mornings, big brother Howard would drive the rest of the kids to school in Theresa Knorr's Ford LTD. Sean would often go along for the ride. The children were always much friendlier in the car, out of reach of their mother.

None of the sisters dated anyone on the street, as they were kept in the house because Theresa Knorr did not want them to get promiscuous. She also refused to give her daughters an allowance.

Sean Martin—whose best friends in the family were Robert and Terry—never tried to date any of the Knorr girls, but his brother Chris was very keen on Sheila for a while, although she did not feel the same way about him. Chris and Sheila even went on a field trip with the school one time, but the relationship never got going.

Sean's family, taking pity on the Knorr children, used to hold birthday parties for them at their house because Theresa Knorr would not allow their friends inside her home.

Inevitably, all the unhappiness inside the Knorr household resulted in Suesan running away from home on a regular basis. The neighbors always knew when she was on her way because there would be a loud commotion outside the house as Suesan ran down the garden path to a waiting gas guzzler filled with her biker-type friends, who would screech off down the street once she'd climbed in.

One time, a bunch of her friends turned up in a station wagon with a Starsky and Hutch stripe down the side. They grabbed Suesan, pushed her in the car and took off at high speed. At first neighbors thought she had been kidnapped, but it later emerged that Suesan had happily gone with them because she could not stand life inside the Knorr house.

Once, Suesan ran away with a practicing satanist. The rest of the family believe the man introduced Suesan to the occult, and that that contributed to her mother's hatred toward her. But a lot of this information was supplied by Theresa Knorr to her children, tempered with exaggerations and lies to ensure that the other brothers and sisters stayed on their mother's side.

There were other recurring problems within the family, like Howard Sanders sexually abusing his half sister Suesan just to get back at his mother. It is not hard to imagine how much influence this had on the dysfunctional situation inside the Knorr household.

Then there was the time all six children were in the backyard of the house on Bellingham, weeding the ground with just a teaspoon each. Howard and his siblings were ordered by Theresa Knorr to completely clear the yard of thistles and weeds and not to go anywhere for four days until they had pulled every one of them out.

The children soaked the ground of the backyard with water before going down on their hands and knees with their spoons. Howard was strong enough to pull the weeds out with his hands, but the others spent hours digging up tiny plots of earth as Theresa Knorr watched from the back window to make sure no one was being lazy.

Not surprisingly, most of the family's neighbors on Bellingham steered clear of the Knorrs, apart from a woman named Cherise Frederick.

Theresa Knorr seemed to have a real friend in Cherise, who was one of the few people ever to be allowed inside the house and actually made to feel relatively welcome.

But Theresa Knorr's real motives in befriending Cherise seemed to be centered around her knowledge of the Bible and religion, and they would spend hours talking about their favorite quotations.

The last couple of years at the house on Bellingham mainly featured a running battle between Suesan and her mother. Suesan was having a lot of emotional problems—besides regularly fleeing the house with her oddball friends, she was not helped by the fact that her mother kept ranting on about her daughter's contract with the devil.

Whenever Suesan acted strangely, Theresa Knorr would tell the other children that Suesan was "up to her usual crap again." She had little or no sympathy for her seemingly disturbed daughter.

Howard tried to stay away from the house on Bellingham because he could not deal with what was going on. But his mother just would not stop going on about Suesan playing with witchcraft and being a devil worshiper.

Howard kept telling his mother that Suesan simply had mental problems. That she needed a doctor. But Theresa Knorr knew best.

At one point, Suesan, then just fifteen, ran away and was arrested by police. She told them about some of the punishments inflicted by her mother, and they took her to the Child Protective Service offices in Sacramento, where she pleaded to be made a ward of court. The CPS even visited the house on Bellingham in response to allegations of parental abuse made by Suesan about her mother.

A number of meetings at the CPS offices followed. But officials did not believe the teenager's story, and her mother was allowed to regain custody of her daughter. Theresa Knorr convinced them that Suesan was just an uncontrollable child, and she assured the CPS she could cope with her. Youngest daughter Terry was forced to lie to CPS officials who visited the house, after being threatened with a beating by her mother. Years later, when police tried to find out the names of the social workers who recommended that Suesan be allowed back home, they were told that all the records had been purged under a five-year rule.

Even the other Knorr children were astonished when Suesan was returned home, since they presumed she would never be allowed to move back into the house on Bellingham.

After Suesan was compelled to move back, it became painfully obvious to Terry that Theresa Knorr was going to punish the teenager even more than before her escape. Her two other daughters were also scared. They could not understand why their mother hated all of them so much.

One day, after years of never being seen, Robert Knorr Sr. visited the house in a bid to see his four children. Theresa Knorr sent Howard's girlfriend Connie—living with Howard at the time—out to talk to Robert Sr. because she knew that he did not know her. Connie had to pretend she was the new owner of the house and that Theresa Knorr and her family had moved on months earlier. Theresa Knorr wanted to prevent Robert Sr. from ever seeing his children again.

During those last few months that the family lived at Bellingham, Howard Sanders was heavily into dealing drugs. Howard contends that Theresa Knorr allegedly knew all about the illicit activities and even helped run the narcotics business in his absence. And when Howard did not have enough cash, he paid his mother the rent in drugs, which she either smoked or made him sell during subsequent drug deals.

One time, Howard was even tipped off by a friend at the Sheriff's Department about a planned raid on the house by private detectives, and cleaned it out of drugs hours before they arrived.

Much of the time, Howard's drugs made the house virtually a pharmacy. Howard was known locally as the mushroom man. He had acid. He had connections for coke, crank, and he always had two different types of weed on him. He also had connections with someone who ripped off pharmacies for speed. He often got the drugs in their sealed bottles straight out of the stores.

With the influx of drug trade to the house came the occasional brush with a number of unsavory characters, who accused Howard Sanders of ripping them off during drug deals.

The Knorr family were warned by some Hell's Angels who lived around the corner that they were going to come over and "rape all the women."

The Angels were angry that Howard had taken away some of their business. Howard even gave his girlfriend Connie that old .22 of his dad's to carry for protection whenever she went to the local store.

Theresa Knorr also frequently issued warnings to Connie, but they had nothing to do with the drug trade. She was concerned about Connie's safety, living under the same roof as her daughter Suesan.

Theresa Knorr told Connie to always lock her bedroom door at night because, she explained coolly, "Suesan is going to try and kill you because she does not like you at all."

Connie was terrified by the threat of murder, especially since she suspected it was partly caused by Suesan's jealousy because Howard had committed incest with her.

But there was another reason why Suesan disliked Connie so much. When she and Connie had been at Pershing Junior High together in Orangevale, Connie and her brother had frequently teased Suesan by calling her "fishface" because she wore big, thick glasses and looked like a nerd.

Suesan Knorr greatly contributed to her reputation as the devil's child within the family by cutting off both her mother's eyelashes, removing bits of her long, spindly fingernails, and stealing a few strands of her waist-length black hair during a daring midnight raid on her mother's dingy bedroom. Theresa Knorr claimed afterward that she did not wake up during the incident because Suesan had drugged her coffee with masses of sleeping tablets.

Theresa Knorr was furious when the children refused to tell their mother who was responsible. She systematically burnt each of them with cigarette butts until they told her who had done the evil deed.

Theresa Knorr knew it was probably Suesan because she suspected that the specimens had been removed for some sort of witchcraft ceremony. She also believed Suesan was jealous of her good looks.

Once Theresa Knorr had confirmed that it was Suesan, it marked the start of a series of horrendous attacks. Theresa Knorr utterly detested her daughter's daring behavior, and she began claiming that Suesan was suffering from sexually transmitted diseases as well.

Shortly afterward, Theresa Knorr told Howard's girl-friend Connie: "She is a witch, and the only way you can kill a witch is by burning them."

Theresa Knorr also warned Connie that anytime she cleaned her hairbrush or trimmed her nails, she should flush it all down the toilet because Suesan could get the remnants and use them for her devil worshiping. Theresa Knorr even ominously told Connie that Suesan would be after her blood eventually.

Even Howard Sanders—hardly a saint by anyone's reckoning—continued to try to get Suesan some discreet medical attention, because he firmly believed she had a mental problem. One day he went over to Connie's stepdad's place on Pershing, in Orangevale, and asked him for advice on how to get his sister committed. But Theresa Knorr once again ignored Howard's pleas when he voiced his concern, and she banned him from ever mentioning the subject again.

The beatings rapidly escalated after the eyelashes incident. Howard Sanders walked in on his mother whipping Suesan with a plastic tube one day. He immediately snatched it curtly from his mother and broke the tube into tiny pieces. But much of the damage had already been done.

Suesan, five feet five inches tall, was approximately the same height as her mother, but Theresa Knorr vastly outweighed her. She had turned into a turtlelike waddler who rocked from side to side as she moved. Her face had become almost square from overeating.

Her expressions, even during the most violent exchanges, ran the gamut from stolid to grave.

Sometimes the violence inflicted on Suesan would subside long enough so that Theresa Knorr could sit her bruised and battered daughter down and make her read excerpts from the Bible. Theresa Knorr also talked about calling in priests to perform exorcisms to get the devil out from within her daughter.

Around this time, Theresa Knorr's drinking increased. She would often keep the children up all night, interrogating them on the different oddities of the Bible.

Theresa Knorr indicated her true feelings about her daughters by always referring to them as "your sisters" during any conversations with the boys. She would spit the words out.

Her possessiveness also knew no boundaries. She tried to encourage her children not to attend school because she wanted to keep an eye on the girls and get the boys out to work from as early an age as possible.

Suesan's last school was Arcade High School, on Watt Avenue, but she only got as far as seventh grade when her mother pulled her out of school, just as she did with Terry a few years later. Sheila managed ninth grade at Casa Robla before she stopped attending.

About the only one who continued with his studies was Billy Bob. By all accounts he had a good head on his shoulders. He was smart and good at sports. The other children believe he stayed in school so much because he was trying to keep out of his mother's reach.

Amazingly, despite all the children's appalling record of

absence from school, no one investigated the family's home life to find out where the problems lay.

Both Robert and Billy Bob had part-time jobs before they turned fifteen, and Billy Bob was extremely bitter about his mother having put all the utilities in his name so that he had to pay for everything out of his modest pay packet. Billy Bob saw it as yet more evidence that his mother was trying to control his life.

It also had a chillingly familiar ring to it. For Theresa Knorr had made every man—including the husband she shot dead—part with his wages the moment he walked through the door.

Four

All happy families resemble one
another; every unhappy family is
unhappy in its own way.
Tolstoy, *Anna Karenina*

Theresa Knorr rocked back and forth in her chair,
Terry recalls. Back and forth. Back and forth. Not a
glint of emotion in her steely blue eyes. Just an empty
stare at the person sitting just a few feet away.

In front of her—crumpled at the kitchen table like a
rag doll incapable, afraid, to defy any order—was her
seventeen-year-old daughter Suesan, whose sin was to
be prettier and thinner than her mother and who was
rumored to be mixing with the devil. It infuriated Theresa Jimmie Knorr to even look at Suesan. She acceler-
ated the pace of her movements on that red rocking
chair. Her eyes locked on Suesan. All the children knew
that was a sign.

The chair creaked under the weight of her 250-pound
frame.

Theresa Knorr pushed a pot filled with macaroni
cheese into her hands.

It was the first of four *boxes of the stuff that she would
make her daughter consume that night.*

Suesan shook as she grabbed the saucepan filled to

46

the brim with food. The scorching hot pot sizzled as it touched the skin of her bare legs.

Suesan's first few mouthfuls brought little response from her mother.

"Don't get that on the floor." Theresa Knorr spat the words out with disgusted contempt.

Suddenly the door to the kitchen burst open and stick-figured, blond Terry rushed in. She stopped dead in her tracks when she saw that her mother was administering her daily dose of punishment to one of her five brothers and sisters.

"Oh! I, uh . . . I didn't mean . . ."

Twelve years old, Terry Knorr looked from her sister Suesan to her mother, then slowly turned her gaze back to her sister with a look of recognition that verged on apathy. Her pallid face seemed to shrink.

"Oh," she repeated dully, taking an involuntary step backward.

It was yet another cruel and twisted moment from within the four battered walls of the Knorr household, but it would remain etched in Terry's memory for the rest of her troubled life.

A few weeks later—in June 1983—Theresa Knorr decided to give her two younger sons—Robert, fourteen, and Billy Bob, fifteen—some lessons in the art of corporal discipline.

Terry recalls that Robert stood behind Suesan at the end of the hall of that comfortable detached home in Orangevale and held her arms back while his brother Billy Bob put on sinister-looking slim black leather bicycle gloves almost like a surgeon preparing for an operation. Theresa Knorr told her son that the gloves were essential for ensuring that no one could detect evidence of the beating Suesan was about to receive.

Theresa Knorr was apparently unhappy because her daughter had not gained enough weight in the previous weeks. No female in that house was going to look prettier and younger than her. And all the devil talk was ringing in her ears.

Then Theresa crashed her own clenched fist deep into her daughter's stomach. The teenager flinched, but dared not utter a sound.

Terry Knorr, having seen more in her short life than most people twice her age, stood behind her mother in the entrance to the main bedroom. Her other sister, Sheila, in the doorway of the bathroom, begged Theresa Knorr to stop.

But neither the mother nor her sons took any notice. Then the two girls saw that their mother had something in her right hand, hanging limply down by the side of her enormous girth. It was a silver pistol with a black plastic handle; a small .22 derringer with a capacity of just two bullets. But one would be enough.

Suesan screamed as she caught sight of that weapon, clutched in her mother's pudgy, pink hands.

Suddenly the whole scene faded to slow motion. Terry watched as her mom lifted her arm and pointed the gun at her sister.

A pop like a champagne cork exploding was the only evidence that she had fired the gun straight at her daughter. The bullet entered underneath her left breast and went right through her rib cage before lodging itself in her back.

Terry watched her sister grab her chest, gasp, then clutch the door frame of the bathroom before stumbling and then falling into the empty bathtub.

An eerie silence enveloped the house for a few seconds as the full impact of what had just occurred sank into the minds of all those present.

Theresa Knorr was the first one to snap out of that trance. She moved swiftly toward her injured daughter.

Clinically, like the nurse she had once been, Theresa Knorr tried to rip the clothes off wounded Suesan. Then she pulled her daughter over the edge of the tub to examine the wound—her only concern was to see precisely where the bullet had entered the body.

That night, Terry and Sheila scrubbed the floor where Suesan had been shot. They scrubbed the door frame where there were bloodstains. They scrubbed every inch of the bathroom apart from the tub where their sister still lay mortally wounded. Theresa Knorr did not have to tell them to do it. They just got on with the task at hand rather than face the wrath of their demonic mother.

Often, the kids would be up until two or three in the morning scrubbing floors and hand-waxing. It was just part of life in that house.

Throughout their entire childhood Theresa Knorr had refused to allow any strangers in the house, because she did not want it dirtied up. In that bathroom, Theresa issued a dire warning to her brood of children: "Just keep your mouths shut. If we have to get rid of the body, we will."

Theresa Knorr was already referring to her daughter Suesan as though she were dead.

Terry wanted to go to the authorities to report the shooting incident, but she feared for her life, so she kept quiet.

Meanwhile, Suesan remained trapped in the bathtub. The other children would regularly creep into the bathroom and stand and stare at her.

Sheila was the one child who bothered to actually talk to her wounded sibling.

Theresa Knorr overheard one conversation between her two daughters during which Sheila spoke about suicide. Minutes later, Terry claims, Theresa Knorr did something that shocked even the boys.

She handed Sheila the very same gun she had just tried to murder her other daughter with, forced it into her shaking hand and said: "If you're so depressed, then kill yourself."

Sheila held tightly onto the gun. Perhaps it was the answer. She walked to her bedroom, lifted the gun to her head and squeezed the trigger. It had no bullets in it . . .

Back in her bathroom prison, Suesan was still somehow surviving despite a massive loss of blood and only a pillow and a blanket for comfort. Amazingly, as the days turned to weeks, she even gradually began to regain her strength.

But the strangest aspect of this already bizarre scenario was that Theresa Knorr started to attend to her injured daughter as if she was the apple of her eye. Lovingly, she dabbed at the half-inch entrance wound where that bullet she had fired so coldly had pierced Suesan through to her back. She even patched the injury with gauze pads. And she regularly fed her daughter antibiotics to stop the infection from spreading. A liberal dose of Flexeril was provided from her secret store of medicines to stop the pain. The drugs all came from hospitals where Theresa had worked years previously.

Theresa could hardly be described as uncommunicative with her children either. She matter-of-factly informed them of the reasons why their sister had to remain in that hellhole of a bathtub. They had no choice, she told her clan. Theresa knew that if there was blood left on anything, then it could easily be traced.

She also did not want to move her daughter, because she didn't know if the bullet would be dislodged. Terry wondered if this was a sign of compassion on the part of her mother (or simply an effort to avoid any further spillages of blood.)

But Terry did not doubt that, having cruelly shot her own daughter, Theresa Knorr turned into a caring nurse, regularly washing her injured daughter and tending to her wounds.

However, at the same time, she forbade the other children from sharing toilet facilities with Suesan by claiming they could catch a disease from her. The real Theresa Knorr was never far away.

As Theresa's clinical attitude continued to be tempered by the occasional sign of warmth, she even told Suesan that she was sorry and asked for forgiveness.

"I forgive you," whispered Suesan.

That was one of many mistakes Suesan made. The beatings would never end.

As the weeks turned into a month, Suesan emerged

from the bathroom having survived a bullet without receiving any professional medical attention. Theresa Knorr was doggedly determined to make sure the authorities never discovered anything about the shooting, even if it had almost cost her daughter her life.

Suesan became a virtual heroine in the eyes of her brothers and sisters. Whenever their mother was out of the room, she faced a stream of questions about the wound. Did the bullet hurt? Did you think you'd die? Terry was even allowed to touch the spot where the bullet had come to a halt after its almost fatal journey through Suesan's body. She could feel it still lodged in her right side.

Theresa Knorr feared that Suesan might try to kill her in revenge for the shooting. She was also worried that her oldest son, Howard, would find out about the incident and decide to punish her. After years under his mother's control, Howard had made a new life for himself outside the vicious web of physical and sexual abuse that had haunted Theresa Knorr and all her children for so many years.

She called Howard up within days of the shooting with a carefully concocted tale deliberately designed to throw him off the scent.

Theresa Knorr told twenty-year-old Howard that Suesan had stabbed her sister Sheila with a steak knife. Sheila—under fear of punishment from her mother—backed up the story dutifully.

Theresa claimed to Howard that a few days later Sheila got hold of the derringer and shot Suesan. The mother reassured her son it had only been a surface wound and she had removed the bullet safely just a short time after the shooting.

Once Suesan had made a recovery—even though she still had the bullet lodged next to her ribs—she tried to keep out of the house on Bellingham Way as much as possible. Frequently she would stay at friends' homes or remain out until late at night.

Howard and his common-law wife Connie moved back into the house when it was up for sale after the shooting. They noticed the scar on Suesan, but the entire family insisted the wound had been inflicted by Sheila, not her mother. Only those in the house on that fateful day knew the truth.

Even Suesan herself backed up this lie by insisting it had been her sister who shot her.

Connie was terrified by Theresa Knorr. One night when she and Howard were living by candlelight in the by-now deserted house in Orangevale, she heard a noise, opened the door to the hallway, and there was Theresa Knorr emptying out a closet. Theresa turned to her and said: "I know what you are. I know what you're doing. You will be punished. Your time will come."

Connie's only two sins in the eyes of Theresa Knorr were to be younger and prettier than her *and* responsible for luring her oldest son away to a new life.

A few weeks later an even more chilling event convinced Connie to try and avoid setting foot inside the Knorr household whenever possible. She was pregnant with her first child by Howard when Theresa Knorr dropped in at Connie's mother's home, which she had moved back to, and informed Connie that Suesan had told her the baby was a boy, would be born on February 1, and he would have a birth defect. All three prophesies came true.

Then Theresa repeated her earlier claims that Suesan had gained special powers after selling her soul to the devil. But, Theresa Knorr insisted, Suesan told her that she was going to kill Connie and the baby because there were not supposed to be any more descendants to carry on the family name. Connie was petrified. She had found herself involved in a very dangerous family.

Five

What did you do that made all of us
turn out so well?
John Wesley, in a letter to his mother
Suzanna

I beat the devil out of you all.
Suzanna Wesley's reply

When Theresa Knorr and her tribe of children moved out of the house in Orangevale to take up residence in a rented cottage just off Auburn Boulevard, on the outskirts of north Sacramento, all the youngsters hoped that it might mark a new violence-free phase in the Knorr household.

The move itself, on October 3, 1983, initiated a reunion between Theresa and her estranged sister Rosemary, whose husband Floyd Norris helped the boys load their U-Haul truck to the brim with furniture for the move to the new place. For years the two sisters had refused to have any contact with each other. No one in the family knew the specific reasons for the feud, but then there had been so many weird incidents over the years, it could have been any of a dozen things.

The single-story property on Auburn was really an annex to the two-story apartment block it was attached to, and many of the residents on that block and in the trailers scattered nearby referred to it as the "laundry room." But the sale of the house in Orangevale had enabled Theresa Knorr to walk away with $50,000 profit, and she was not about to fritter it away on some fancy home. At $280 a month, the Auburn house was a bargain.

Other children on the block soon got to know the Knorr kids, and some were surprised by their attitude toward their mother when her back was turned.

Billy Bob frequently described his mother as nutty and weird to neighbor William Hall. And Theresa Knorr showed herself to have a distinct lack of a sense of humor after Hall stopped to pass the time of day with her and somehow ended up getting around to the subject of Adam and Eve. When Hall joked, "That was a classic case of incest," Theresa Knorr walked off in a huff, obviously deeply offended.

But within a few months Theresa Knorr made up with the Halls and became quite friendly with the young family. She even gave them a painting of a fountain scene for Christmas. The Halls—suspicious that there might be an underlying influence of satanism inside the Knorr household—became convinced the picture was in some way cursed, and eventually Bill's wife made him take it off the wall because she believed it would bring them bad luck.

Suesan—the bullet still firmly lodged in her back—was still trying to keep out of her mother's way, but life proved even more terrifying for her inside the new house. Theresa Knorr had deliberately chosen a smaller property so she could keep an even closer eye on her clan. She was especially determined to control every aspect of Suesan's life. Since the shooting, Theresa had continued to decide when and where her daughter should eat. She was banned from joining the others at mealtimes for days on end.

Within a few days of the family moving into the house just off Auburn Boulevard, Theresa Knorr produced a pair of police regulation handcuffs bought at a pawnshop at nearby Del Paso Boulevard and ordered Suesan to put socks over her hands so the manacles would not leave any marks on her wrists. Later, she introduced canvas wrist restraints because, despite the preventive measures, definite marks could be seen on Suesan's wrists.

Suesan complied with her mother's orders because she knew she would be beaten either by her mother or brother Billy Bob if she disobeyed.

Theresa Knorr also regularly blindfolded Suesan with a silk scarf from her vast selection of scarves, collected since the early seventies, when they were considered fashionable.

Suesan was the child most feared by Theresa Knorr. She was still regularly muttering about her daughter being sent by the devil, and she always insisted that at least one of the other children stand guard over her. They were told that if Suesan got out of the house, they were in big trouble, and they knew what that meant.

Theresa Knorr's other main motive for keeping Suesan prisoner was to prevent her repeating that previous trip she had made to the Child Protection Services in Sacramento.

Once, when Theresa went on a rare shopping trip with her newfound fortune from selling the house in

Orangevale, Terry was left at home with Suesan and her brother Robert. Theresa had not fed Suesan for a couple of days and she was weak. Terry went into the kitchen and got her a glass of water with sugar in it so that it would help bring her blood sugar back up. Diabetes ran in the family, and Terry thought that her sister might have been diabetic. Also, there was no food in the house, so she could not give her anything more substantial.

Talk of black magic and Suesan's so-called dangerous powers continued to dominate Theresa Knorr's conversation inside the house off Auburn Boulevard. None of the children dared question their mother's rantings. By this time, Terry recalls, Suesan was so battered and bruised by her mother and brothers that her appearance was physically altered. In the eyes of her family, that was yet more evidence of the devil within her.

After handcuffing her to her bed each night, Theresa Knorr allegedly fed her daughter Mellaril tranquilizers to keep her sedated to prevent her from getting hysterical.

At night the other children lay terrified in their beds as weird voices emanated from Suesan. There were dozens of different tones and accents; deep, throaty roars; high-pitched screams; constant mumbling in Spanish. It was more like a scene out of *The Exorcist* than family life in a suburban California town.

Theresa Knorr told the others that Suesan had to be locked up, as she was trying to kill her sister Sheila because she was a virgin and she wanted to use Sheila for a human sacrifice.

And, Theresa insisted, Suesan was still sometimes feeding her huge doses of sleeping pills in her drinks at night, and she believed she was going to try and kill her. Theresa was also convinced that her daughter's illness had caused her own excessive weight gain, intestinal problems, stomachaches, headaches, and high blood pressure. She insisted Suesan was deliberately making her sick because she had signed her name in blood and sold her soul to the devil.

To the outside world, Theresa Knorr's ailments sound more like the classic symptoms of hypochondria. But in that household no one ever questioned her words of wisdom.

Murders in the sprawling blue-collar suburbs of Sacramento are not all that rare, so the violent, tragic death of Theresa Knorr's sister Rosemary on November 30, 1983, caused no more than a ripple of interest in the city.

Inside the Knorr household off Auburn Boulevard it was very much the same story. It was as if the brutality that ruled the lives of Theresa Knorr and her flock of children had neutralized any real emotions when it came to anything that happened outside those four walls.

The *Sacramento Bee* daily newspaper followed police inquiries into Rosemary Norris's murder in the suburb of Roseville with only a sprinkling of interest. Reading between the lines of the newspaper's published reports, it seemed as if her demise was considered a low-life trailer-trash-type crime. Who cared?

A piece on page 6 headlined INVESTIGATORS FINALLY

IDENTIFY WOMAN STRANGLED IN PLACER on December 2, 1983, seemed to say it all:

AUBURN—The Placer County Sheriff's Department identified Thursday the strangled woman whose body was left on a dead-end road in southern Placer County as Rosemary Norris, 39, of Citrus Heights.

An autopsy Thursday found that Norris died of "manual strangulation," Sheriff Don Nunes said.

A Rocklin man found the body while walking his dog in the Sunset-Whitney industrial area between Roseville and Rocklin, Nunes said.

Investigators found no tracks or any sign there had been a struggle at the scene. "Her body temperature (when found) would suggest that she was only recently deposited there," Nunes said.

Officials are looking for a missing 1967 white-and-blue GMC truck which belonged to Norris.

However, despite the *Bee*'s low-key projection of the murder, homicide detectives were naturally determined to find the killer.

Rosemary Norris had last been seen by friends at her Castillo Court home at 4:30 P.M. on the day she disappeared. Unlike her lazier, younger sister, she had worked for many years at the state's Department of Finance headquarters in Sacramento. She was the success story in the family.

Her husband, Floyd Norris Jr., had reported Rosemary missing to the Sacramento County Sheriff's Department when he returned home the following day from a business trip.

Privately, detectives suspected who might be responsible for the killing, but they needed more evidence before they could even consider issuing an arrest warrant.

"Do you mind if I come in to ask you a few questions about the death of your sister?"

Detective Johnnie Smith had a hunch that Theresa Knorr might know something about her sister's killing, so he called at the house just off Auburn Boulevard, in mid-December 1983.

The detective suspected there might have been some sort of relationship between Rosemary's husband and Theresa because he had been spending a lot of time at the house.

Smith did not notice anything wrong inside that house when he sat down in the living room to interview Theresa Knorr. He saw all the children, except Suesan. And Theresa Knorr even struck him as a caring mother.

Theresa was charming to the visiting policeman. She told Smith a sob story about how her sister considered her the black sheep of the family because she had been married so many times. Smith never once heard Suesan Knorr whimpering, and he certainly had no idea she may have been manacled to a table in the kitchen while he was in the house.

The only thing that stuck in the detective's mind was that Theresa Knorr looked very strange at the time, with her black, greasy hair down to her waist and very overweight. But he also noted the children were coming and going in a relaxed manner.

"I have thought about this so many times since," he said ten years later. "I thought about whether there was something I should have detected. Was there some problem? But I was there on an entirely different matter."

Smith left the house that day none the wiser as far as his investigation into the murder of Rosemary Norris was concerned. Theresa Knorr had tactfully answered all his questions, but provided him with no fresh clues as to the identity of the killer.

Three months later, in mid-March 1984, two men sitting in their four-door sedan did not even merit a glance in the busy roadway that led to the apartment block attached to the house, just off Auburn Boulevard.

They watched four of the Knorr children coming and going without even questioning the fact that one daughter never seemed to emerge from the house. But then that was not the purpose of the Placer County Sheriff's Department surveillance operation.

Their job was to observe the movements of Floyd Norris Jr. following his wife's mysterious death. It was a last ditch effort to try and pin the murder on the husband. They were still intrigued by his continual visits to his sister-in-law's home. Perhaps they were having an affair, as police had suspected months earlier? Or maybe they were involved in some business scheme or other? Whatever the reasons behind Norris's trips to Auburn Boulevard, Detective Johnnie Smith wanted some answers, and since Floyd was not talking, a watching and waiting game was their only option.

For more than three days Smith and his partner observed Floyd's movements, completely unaware of the fear and injury being inflicted by Theresa Knorr on her children inside that very house. As it happened, antique dealer and furniture restorer Norris was reupholstering some chairs for his sister-in-law, and that seems to have been the only motive behind his regular visits. Unknown to everyone at the time, Theresa Knorr had had another falling out with her sister just a few weeks before her murder, following a row concerning some money Rosemary loaned to her sister. But Theresa was and never has been a suspect in the death of Rosemary Norris.

Detective Smith later conceded that Floyd Norris had been a suspect, but detectives never uncovered any evidence that would pin it on him.

Floyd Norris moved to Reno sometime after his wife's death, and police have completely lost track of him.

Six

Whoever strikes his father or mother
shall be put to death.
Exodus 21:15

Whoever curses his father or mother
shall be put to death.
Exodus 21:17

With the arrival of spring, life inside that small house off Auburn Boulevard continued to go from bad to worse for Theresa Knorr's daughters.

Terry remembers that by this time her mother was convinced that not only had Suesan given her a fatal illness, but her daughter was also suffering from venereal disease, which Theresa Knorr was in danger of catching if she did not take certain preventive measures.

Just after the police surveillance of the house ended, Theresa Knorr decided to ban Suesan from sharing the same toilet with the rest of the family for fear of getting VD from her. Unlike the house at Bellingham, there was only one toilet in their new home.

Suesan continued to be handcuffed to her bed each night. Theresa Knorr tended to make the manacles doubly tight on evenings when there was a full moon, according to the other children.

Gradually, the energy and health that Suesan had battled so bravely to regain following that shooting the previous year was being drained out of her body. Theresa Knorr seemed to take a perverse delight in watching her daughter slowly disintegrate in front of her very eyes. The move to Auburn Boulevard was in effect the final nail in Suesan Knorr's coffin . . .

One night, Theresa Knorr made Suesan stand with her back to her in the tiny kitchen. Suesan was so sick with fever by this stage that she was virtually a walking zombie, too weak to argue with anybody about anything.

Theresa Knorr allegedly picked up a pair of scissors and aimed them at her daughter's back as if she were about to throw a dart into a board. The scissors embedded at least an inch into their target. Suesan stood there in silence, and Theresa looked admiringly at her handiwork. A few moments later she pulled them out of her daughter's back without a word, treated the wound with gauze padding, and then ordered her to her bedroom, where she was handcuffed and blindfolded once more. Naturally, there would be no calls to doctors. No professional medical advice. Theresa Knorr would take care of it all. And no one ever dared ask her what the sick and twisted reason behind that attack had been.

It was exactly the same story a few weeks later when she stood on Suesan's neck as punishment for some sin or other. Youngest sister Terry watched as Suesan—convulsing on the floor—was crushed underfoot by Theresa Knorr's enormous frame.

Susan Sullivan—who lived in the apartment block attached to the Knorr house—took pity on young Terry and regularly let her come to her apartment to watch television.

But two incidents occurred that sparked some problems. The first was when Terry visited Susan's apartment one day, and a few hours later Susan Sullivan noticed a pair of earrings missing.

She went to speak to Theresa Knorr about the missing items, and shortly afterward Theresa came back up to Susan's apartment and gave her another pair of earrings, which clearly implied that the others had been stolen by Terry.

But Susan Sullivan was even more concerned when the attractive teenager started flirting with a male friend of hers, who was eighty years old.

"She started to get real over-chummy with this guy. It got to the point where I started to say 'hold on there young lady.' " explained Susan.

"I decided there and then I did not want her around anymore. I did not trust her. Maybe it was the lack of a father around the house that made her so overfriendly with my guy. But she kept brushing against him, smiling at him real seductively and flirting with him the whole time. In the end I just gave her and the rest of the family the cold shoulder."

A few miles away across town—on June 1, 1984—Theresa Knorr's oldest son, Howard, married live-in lover Connie, but sadly, they were not destined to live happily ever after. Their relationship was in trouble even before the wedding.

Connie believes her marriage to Howard was ruined by his mother's influence because he attempted to exert the same type of control over her. Connie says she suffered numerous beatings at the hands of her abusive ex-husband. He even spent a year in jail for one attack in the late 1980s.

Connie filed a list of incidents with spousal abuse agencies in Sacramento, including when she alleged Howard beat his baby son, Howard Jr., before going out on a drug run. Soon after, she fled the house they shared, filed divorce proceedings, and sought full custody of their two children.

In 1990, Howard was arrested after making threats to hire someone to kill his wife. Connie says she dropped the charges after getting scared. She also claimed that Howard boasted to her about beating a boy when he was a youngster at school.

To Connie, Howard had become like a robot on behalf of his mother. Even after the Knorrs moved out of that house on Bellingham, Theresa would call Howard everytime she had a problem with the children and ask him to come over and help teach them a lesson.

July 5, 1984, was one of those rare evenings when there was no screaming, no abuse, no stabbings, and no shootings inside the Knorr household. The atmosphere was about as laid-back as anyone could remember. The lull before the storm . . .

The main cause of all this, according to Terry, was the pungent whiff of cannabis that wafted across the living room of the cottage. Sitting on a couch, like two giggling students, were Theresa Knorr and Suesan, the daughter she had abused so horrifically.

Taking an enormous drag of the fat, badly rolled joint, Theresa Knorr gazed almost lovingly at her battered daughter before exhaling a vast cloud of mustardy smoke.

Daughter Terry, just thirteen years old at the time, watched her mother and sister taking those illicit drugs, convinced it was proof that perhaps her mother still had some sense of reality left in her mind. It was ironic that mind-altering substances might actually be responsible for cleansing Theresa Knorr's soul . . . albeit temporarily.

Terry was amazed that her mother and Suesan—the object of so many vicious attacks—were actually talking together like a mother and daughter should. Suesan was yet again playing her role as the ultimate human sponge, prepared to soak up vicious attacks and virtually constant imprisonment, in exchange for the very occasional evidence of a loving, caring mother.

The cannabis also influenced Suesan to make one last desperate attempt to escape her hellhole. It was anesthetizing all that pain sufficiently so that she managed to beg her mother to let her leave home. Anything. Any life outside that house seemed preferable to what she had just gone through.

"Just buy me a plane ticket, send me to Alaska, I'll be a prostitute on the pipeline. I don't care, I just want to leave," a very stoned Suesan told her mother.

Equally stoned, Theresa Knorr had actually allowed the pot to mellow her rigidity. She announced she would allow her daughter to leave home—but there was one condition. Suesan would have to let her mother remove that bullet still lodged in her back.

Through the clouds of cannabis smoke it seemed a reasonable request. For the first time since being shot

Suesan could see just a glint of light at the end of that awful tunnel. Having that bullet removed was going to be Suesan's ticket to freedom.

The reason Theresa insisted on taking out the bullet before freeing her daughter, Terry told police, was because she knew it was evidence of the crime she had committed against her daughter. She was afraid she could be traced by the bullet. Some years earlier her guns had been taken by the police and ballistic tests done on them, and she believed they could be traced back to her.

One of the detectives investigating the Knorr case ten years later asked Terry what would have happened if Suesan had just got up and walked out of that house.

"Suesan would have ended up dead," came the cold reply.

The surgery to remove Suesan's bullet, as described by Terry, resembled a scene out of *Frankenstein*. Terry played the role of doctor's assistant, but in reality her job was more like anesthetist/assistant surgeon/nurse all wrapped into one.

However, this was no operating theater. This was the kitchen of a tiny, overcrowded house, and there was not even a gurney in sight. Instead, just a slab of floor where Suesan was told to lie in preparation for her surgery. A pillow was placed under her stomach so that it would be taut enough for surgery to commence.

A couple of medical instruments lay idly nearby on the sideboard. Suesan was fed a handful of tiny green Mellaril painkillers, but it was a gallon bottle of Old

Crow that would become the Knorr equivalent of anesthetic.

Before positioning her daughter for what in anyone's terms was major surgery, Theresa Knorr thrust that vast jug of whiskey into her daughter's lap and ordered her to drink it. Unlike the macaroni cheese all those months earlier, this was one command that Suesan believed was actually in her own interests.

Suesan rapidly swallowed back about half of the Old Crow before she was knocked out cold.

Meanwhile, Theresa peeled on a pair of rubber surgical gloves, making sure to stretch them professionally before squeezing them over those short, stubby fingers. She ordered her two sons, Billy Bob and Robert, to hold their sister down. Then she grabbed a scalpel and a pair of pincers, and got to work. She had stolen everything from her earlier jobs in convalescent hospitals.

Two hours later Theresa finally succeeded in digging the bullet out of her daughter's back. Suesan had lost enormous quantities of blood, but that did not seem to concern her mother. Her main objective was to remove the evidence that could have resulted in her being prosecuted for attempted murder.

From the moment she extracted that slug, she grasped onto it, not even daring to set it down for a second, in case it disappeared. She did not trust any of her children—she suspected they would turn her in if given half a chance.

Suesan was still knocked out cold. Her face was twisted to the side, pressed hard on the cold kitchen floor. Her back arched at a grotesque angle. Somehow she was still breathing.

Theresa said nothing. Her assistant, Terry, was so dumbfounded that she could not speak . . .

Luckily for Suesan, she did not recover consciousness until the next day. Although some members of the family believe that she would have been better off if she had never woken up.

When Suesan did awake, she was still severely groggy and her body remained facedown on the floor, growing weaker and more feverish with each passing hour. Theresa Knorr ordered the other children to simply step around or over Suesan whenever they were in the kitchen.

She would not even allow the rest of the family to help Suesan to the bathroom. Theresa Knorr simply ordered Billy Bob and Robert to place diapers beneath Suesan's pelvis and change them when the smell of urine and feces got too overpowering in the summer heat.

Theresa fed her daughter constant antibiotics to keep infection from setting in, and she gave her ibuprofen and Motrin for the inflammation.

But Suesan was deteriorating fast. A week after the operation, she started hallucinating and began calling her brother William, "Grandpa."

"I can see my life passing before my eyes," Suesan told her baby sister Terry.

Then lockjaw set in . . .

"She was dying. I just know," says Terry today. "It was like a movie, you know . . ."

The other sister, Sheila, was so concerned she actually plucked up the courage to confront her mother: "Suesan's dying. We gotta do something."

"What d'you want me to do about it? I've tried to help her. There's nothing more I can do," came the terse reply from the only parent in that household.

Theresa Knorr allegedly conceded that her daughter did need proper medical attention, but she strictly forbade any attempt to call in a doctor, for fear it would expose her. When she wanted to see if Suesan was still alive, she kicked her and listened for a groan.

"She needs a doctor, she needs to go to a hospital, but if I take her to a hospital, she's been beaten so badly that I'm gonna go to jail. We can't do that."

The children were told to sit with their sister and keep an eye on her all night long.

Seven

> When the child recovers from the attack, he feels enormously confused, in fact, split—innocent and culpable at the same time—and the confidence in the testimony of his own senses is broken. To survive this ordeal, the child has to register the bad . . . as good.
> Albert Shengold, child care expert

On the evening of July 12, 1984, police would later charge, Theresa Knorr walked into the children's bedroom, sat down on one of the bunk beds, and announced to her sons and Sheila that she had come up with a solution on what to do with Suesan, who was still sprawled out on the kitchen floor. Her wound had become so badly infected that the skin had turned pink, then bright red all around the gaping sore.

Terry—keeping guard over Suesan in the kitchen—could not avoid staring at her sister's eyes. Her adolescent curiosity was getting the better of her. Suesan's once pretty, sparkling blue eyes had transformed to a pale, yellowing greenish color in a matter of days.

Theresa Knorr later told one family member that her daughter's change of eye color had been caused by the devil. She told her daughter-in-law Connie that Suesan was definitely a witch. She insisted that the only way to kill a witch was to burn them.

As Terry stared at her sister, her eyes panned down and noticed a rib almost poking through Suesan's stomach and hundreds of black marks on her back.

With just an undersized diaper around her waist, Suesan Knorr was actually experiencing less dignity in life than death.

The following day, Theresa Knorr began her preparations for the scheme she had been planning with Sheila and the boys. First she went and bought a red, one-gallon gas can. Then she filled her son's yellow 1978 Mercury Cougar—known around the Knorr household as the pimp mobile—with gas.

Terry watched her mother pack the gas can in the trunk of the Mercury, together with a large box of six-inch-long Blue Diamond wooden matches. She also saw Theresa put all of Suesan's belongings into a plastic Glad garbage bag and load that into the car as well; clothes, jewelry, purses, belts, shoes.

The final proof of what was about to happen came when Terry witnessed her mother performing an extraordinary ritual in the yard behind the house.

"I watched her take olive oil. It was her little God ritual thing. She took olive oil, poured it over my sister's pictures. She pulled every picture she had of my sister, and she burnt them," Terry later explained.

Back inside the house, Suesan was being dressed up by her brothers and sister Sheila. They put her clothes on her like a toddler being prepared for school. First they struggled to get her into a dark-colored corduroy jumpsuit with a hood. Then followed white sneakers and a ski-jacket-style coat.

It was past midnight on July 15 when Theresa Knorr, her two sons, and her daughter Sheila were finally ready to depart. Youngest daughter Terry pleaded desperately with her mother to be allowed to join them on their trip. Theresa had already admitted she was going to get rid of Suesan. The boys told her they were going to set her alight someplace in the mountains.

Terry feared being left alone in the house. But Theresa rejected her pleas. She did not want her youngest daughter to see the sacrifice of her sister.

"Loose lips sink ships," she told Terry.

In the background, groaning on the kitchen floor, was helpless Suesan, a constant stream of incoherent babbling coming from between her lips. Everything was slurred. She was mumbling.

Just before they took her out, Terry leaned down and whispered in her sister's ear: *"I love you."*

In another room, Theresa Knorr was getting the car keys and her purse as if she was rushing out to get to the local store before it closed.

Robert and William crouched down on either side of Suesan and pulled her up, holding her arms. Suesan had drop foot and they had to drag her across the floor, her feet hanging limply behind her. She could not walk. She wasn't even attempting to.

Terry was then ordered to hold the front seat of the two-door car forward while they stuck Suesan in the backseat. Her head slumped onto Sheila's lap and then her knees were pulled over Robert's lap. It was one hell of a squash by all accounts, as the Cougar was not a big car. Up front Billy Bob and his mother, who drove, sank into the bucket seats.

Terry watched as the Cougar purred along the narrow track toward the exit from the trailer park complex, and then she returned to the empty house terrified. Fear and paranoia ran rampant through her confused mind.

Two hours later the distinct rumble of the Cougar's V8 alerted Terry that her family had returned. Theresa Knorr walked in mumbling something about the engine in William's car knocking. Their plan had been aborted at the last moment. Suesan Knorr's death sentence had been commuted . . . for a few hours at least. She was returned to her miserable home on the kitchen floor, too delirious to realize that the family had already agreed to restart their mission the following evening.

Theresa Knorr and Billy Bob announced they were exhausted following their late night excursion, and retired for a nap in the bunk beds in the children's room. Theresa, far too heavy to manage to clamber up to the top bunk, took the bottom bed.

Billy Bob, as Terry always called him, hardly ever got spanked by his mother. Theresa Knorr's blatant favoritism toward him was the result of Billy Bob's remarkable resemblance to how Robert Knorr Sr. looked when he was in the Marines and first swept Theresa off her feet.

Early the next evening, the brothers were ordered to transfer all Suesan's belongings to Theresa's car, a maroon 1978 Ford LTD with a white vinyl top. It was a strange-looking vehicle, a two-door sedan in the body of a four-door limo, complete with wire spoke wheels and whitewall tires. Terry never forgot those whitewall tires because her mother made her clean and polish the scruffy car so perfectly.

That night, Terry was once again ordered to play the role of prison guard on Suesan as she lay dying on the kitchen floor.

At one point during the evening, the terrified thirteen-year-old actually thought her sister had died. She got down next to the body on her knees and shook her and talked to her. At first there was no response. She repeated her actions. Suesan started babbling nonsense again. It was like music to Terry's ears because it meant she was still alive.

Terry continued her round-the-clock guard duty until about midnight, when the family plan was reignited. This time Terry did not plead to join them. Her instincts told her it would be better not to play any part in their dreadful scheme.

Theresa Knorr carefully reversed the car along the side of the house before they carried Suesan out of the back door dressed in the same jumpsuit. They placed her in exactly the same position in the Ford LTD as they had in the Cougar the previous evening.

Terry studied her brothers and sisters for any signs of emotion. Robert seemed really twitchy, while Billy Bob was calm and cool, showing no fear. Theresa Knorr was the same. But Sheila was shaking.

Theresa and her clan drove up Interstate 80, northeast toward Reno. About sixty miles out of Sacramento, just beyond the Donner Pass, Theresa turned south on state Highway 89 and headed for the winter ski resort of Squaw Valley. In the summer months it wasn't nearly so popular, and it didn't take long to find a secluded spot near Squaw Creek. There, they unloaded the pile of Suesan's belongings and fashioned a makeshift bier. They set Suesan on top of it. Then Billy Bob doused her with generous amounts of gasoline. Theresa Knorr waddled back to the car and started the engine. She watched as her son lit a match and dropped it on the bier and ran back to the car.

"If you ever tell anybody about this, you're going to be next," Theresa told Billy Bob as he climbed back into the Ford LTD.

The drive back to Auburn Boulevard at dawn that morning was carried out in virtually complete silence. But one incident occurred that terrified Theresa and her children more than the murder of their own flesh and blood.

Suddenly, as they powered along Highway 89, a bird smashed into the windshield of the Ford LTD, almost shattering it. Theresa was so thrown by the incident she swerved the car dangerously and almost lost control. Sheila was screaming. All the occupants of the car that sweltering night were convinced of one thing—that bird had committed suicide on the windshield. Theresa Knorr told her children it was a sign—"an offering or a sacrifice."

They presumed the bird was the soul of Suesan come to say good-bye forever.

The following morning, July 17, the family returned to the house off Auburn Boulevard minus Suesan. Theresa Knorr and her sons were keen to tell little Terry all the graphic details.

They told her how they left Suesan in a beautiful area that was surrounded by trees, and there was a little clearing, like a meadow, as if to reassure her that her sister's final resting place was so pretty it was the perfect place to die.

Theresa explained to Terry how Billy Bob pulled Suesan out of the car, laid her down, then, with Robert, pulled all her belongings out and spread them all around her. Robert then got back in the car, where Sheila sat terrified.

"When they poured gas over her and they got to about her chest area, her lower face area, it was like her —her entire body just collapsed, just like her soul was leaving her body," Terry later recalled them telling her.

Theresa even reassured Terry that her sister had already died before the blaze was started.

"That's when her soul escaped the corpse," she chillingly added.

Howard Sanders—the only member of Theresa Knorr's family to have actually escaped the nest before the death of Suesan—read an article in the *Bee* about a body found burning near Tahoe City just a few days later. It instantly reminded his wife Connie of those chilling conversations with her mother-in-law some weeks earlier when she had talked about having Suesan exorcised.

Howard carefully studied every word of the article, which reported that authorities had found the body off Highway 89 and presumed it was a woman who had a child because of the diapers scattered near the body. Howard suspected it must have been his half sister.

Howard confronted his mother on the phone, but she just said, simply, that Suesan had gone. Howard, understandably stunned, tried to question his mother further, but she repeated that she had gone. When he pressed her once again, she admitted Suesan was dead, but refused to elaborate. Instead she promised her oldest son she would tell him about it some other time.

When Howard did next see his mother, she insisted that Suesan had died of natural causes. But she refused to go into much detail. Howard did not believe his mother, and later confronted his two brothers, Robert and Billy Bob, about the article in the *Bee*. Robert admitted the body referred to was Suesan but added cryptically: "She was literally rotting away alive anyhow."

When Howard was living with his in-laws on Pershing Avenue, Orangevale, Theresa Knorr dropped by unexpectedly one afternoon and insisted her son go in the Ford LTD with her.

Howard was terrified of his mother because of what he suspected had happened to Suesan. He was afraid that she might kill him if he asked too many questions about Suesan.

Howard was particularly spooked by the menacing-looking pair of tight red leather driving gloves his mother was wearing when she picked him up that day. Red was her favorite color. He was convinced she was using them to avoid getting her fingerprints on anything.

Paranoia was running rampant through Theresa Knorr's family—much of it inspired by her allegedly brutal regime.

Shortly after Suesan's death, Terry, just thirteen, made the first of many attempts to run away from the dreadful place she called home. She took off to live with a gang of youths in their late teens in a run-down apartment block a short distance from Auburn Boulevard. Theresa Knorr was furious when she heard, and immediately ordered eldest son Howard to go and get her back with the aid of his younger brother, Billy Bob.

The two brothers went over to the building on Marconi where they had heard Terry was staying, to find a party in full swing. Howard banged on the door and heard Terry say: "Oh shit, it's my brother." She then ran out the back door, and a bunch of heavyset bikers rushed out the front and tried to pick a fight with Howard and Billy Bob.

Howard cooled the potentially dangerous situation by talking to the men, but he never actually persuaded Terry to come home. However, a few weeks later she arrived back at the house off Auburn Boulevard and all was forgiven . . . for the time being.

Eight

> "There's a light above me. I think it's a
> hole. I'm gonna climb toward it."
> Sheila Sanders, three days before she
> died

February 17, 1985, was a bleak and chilly night on
Fulton Avenue, in the Del Paso Heights area of Sacramento. Tatty mid-seventies gas guzzlers cruised close to
the sidewalk with their full beams turned up to high-
light the prostitutes advertising their bodies in exchange
for the cost of a set of retreads. Their lights illuminated
black leather skirts, assorted stilettos, and white knee-
high boots on a three-inch heel. But whatever the pack-
aging, the end result was the same.

Theresa Knorr's twenty-year-old daughter Sheila had
allegedly only recently started working Fulton Avenue
after some heavy pressure from her mother. Theresa
demanded that each of her surviving children give her
most of their earnings from whatever jobs—legal or ille-
gal—they might have.

No one knows what Sheila really thought about working as a prostitute. It just wasn't a topic of conversation
inside the Knorr household. When Theresa Knorr demanded that she pay her keep, Sheila at first started
streetwalking on Auburn Boulevard, just two minutes

from their house. But the clients who drifted along that red-light district rarely paid more than ten dollars a trick. The good money was over at Fulton. Word on the street was that car salesmen and the businessmen who owned the dozens of trailer parks in the area would happily pay as much as two hundred bucks for a few hours in a nearby motel room with a girl.

Youngest daughter Terry could not understand why her half sister did not run away once she had earned some cash from turning tricks on Fulton. Terry certainly would have left home if given half the chance. In her mind, getting up to $200 for each trick was the sort of big money that would provide a route out of that terrible household.

Life inside Theresa Knorr's home was also difficult for Sheila for other reasons. She did not want to be a prostitute forever, and she was dating one local guy seriously, even considering marriage. But she could not ask her boyfriend back to the house—let alone mention the word marriage in front of her mother—without risking a terrible beating.

Sheila regularly ended up with two black eyes in one session following a thrashing by Theresa and her boys. But Sheila did not once attempt to run away—however unpleasant life became, she seemed to stay out of some misplaced loyalty toward the family.

Meanwhile, Theresa Knorr had banned the very mention of deceased daughter Suesan after becoming occasionally and uncharacteristically haunted by her memory. Theresa admitted sometimes feeling a cold draft up her back when she walked by Suesan's closet.

She believed that her daughter's soul had come back to haunt her.

However, police would later charge that none of this stopped Theresa Knorr from turning her brutal attentions toward Sheila. One day she beat her up after accusing her of getting pregnant by one of the many men who paid her for sex over at Fulton.

Over the next few weeks, Theresa Knorr became increasingly obsessed about Sheila's "pregnancy," even though there was no actual evidence she was expecting a child.

Things reached a head late one night when Theresa made Sheila cycle to the store more than half a mile away on Auburn Boulevard, to pick up some cigarettes.

Bicycling furiously past the leery eyes of the transvestites and rent boys plying for trade on the strip of Auburn known as the meatrack, Sheila must have wondered where her life was leading. There was no escape from Sacramento's thriving cash-for-sex scene, even while out on an errand for her mother.

But as she pedaled past the imposing entrance to the Lombard Mortuary, a motorist rammed into her bike, knocking her to the ground. The driver did not even stop to see if she was okay. But then that was typical of life on the rougher side of town.

Sheila was taken by paramedics to the nearby Mercy Hospital, in Sacramento. For once the bruises and cuts had not been inflicted at home, but any hope that Theresa Knorr might actually offer some sympathy soon disappeared.

Her mother was concerned about the accident. But her worries had nothing to do with Sheila's injuries. She believed that the incident was a sign from above. A sign that indicated her daughter had been taken over by the devil.

Theresa was convinced that when Sheila got hit in front of that mortuary, she had died and a demon took over her body, or so she told the rest of the family.

However, there was worse to come.

Theresa still believed that Sheila was pregnant. That combination of twisted opinions sparked a tirade of abuse that was even more horrendous than anything Suesan had suffered the previous year before her death.

Within minutes of struggling back into the house from the hospital, Sheila was being held by her brothers Billy Bob and Robert while her mother gave her a serious beating.

Theresa Knorr, once of the delicate chin and wispy brown hair, was certainly no longer slender and easy on the eyes. She weighed 250 pounds and had her hair pulled back like a sumo wrestler. Her features were bloated. Her arms were the size of Popeye's, and her once-pretty waistline was now as thick and elastic as a truck tire. And she packed enormous power in each of those punches.

Sheila's body soon turned black and blue from where Theresa had beaten and strangled her. The nightmare was back on course, and that evening's proceedings had only just begun.

According to Terry, after smashing Sheila around for a while, Theresa Knorr started force-feeding Sheila with macaroni cheese, just as she had done to Suesan. Some old habits never die, they come back to haunt you forever.

On that same horrendous night, Theresa also managed to break Sheila's front tooth off while trying to force-feed her the macaroni. As the food was shoveled down her throat, she even started vomiting.

Theresa then decided that measures needed to be taken to prevent anyone from seeing some of her daughter's dreadful injuries. She forced Sheila to sit in the bathtub while she filled it with cold water and ice cubes. Then she made her stay in it for upward of an hour in an effort to bring out the bruising she had just inflicted on her daughter.

From then on Theresa Knorr also began handcuffing Sheila to the underneath of the kitchen table at night so she could not escape. They were the same cuffs that had been used to such chilling effect on her sister less than a year earlier.

As an afterthought, Theresa called up lawyer Wes Seegmiller to help push for a claim off the insurance company following Sheila's accident. Theresa Knorr never liked to miss out on an opportunity to make some extra cash.

But another matter was particularly aggravating Theresa at that time. Her beloved teenage son Billy Bob had dared to announce he was leaving home to move into an apartment on run-down Fulton Boulevard with a pretty teenage girl called Emily Lewis, who worked with him at the movie theater on Ethan Way.

Theresa was infuriated that her favorite son was striking out on his own. Billy Bob told dark-haired Emily that he had been kicked out of home by his mom—nothing could have been further from the truth. But whatever his excuse, Billy Bob managed to persuade

Emily to set up home with him, and he even took on another part-time job at Arco Arena and worked a third job at a book company in West Sacramento, to ensure he could afford the rent on the apartment.

Emily never went into the Knorr family home just off Auburn throughout the nine months she lived with Billy Bob. He told her that one of his sisters had run away and he openly admitted he did not care much for either Sheila or Suesan. Emily never questioned why Billy Bob was so obsessed with not allowing her inside the family house.

She did feel there was something unusual about the family, and it worried her, but she could not actually fathom what the problem was.

With Theresa Knorr's obsession about Sheila's pregnancy growing every day, her eldest daughter was unshackled and allowed to go—under the escort of her two brothers, naturally—to a local doctor to establish once and for all if she was actually expecting a child.

When it was confirmed that she wasn't pregnant, Theresa still continued to insist Sheila had venereal disease. So she made her go to another doctor to be checked for chlamydia and pelvic inflammatory disease.

Theresa Knorr even took her own penicillin to fight off the diseases she was convinced she had caught from her daughter. She then started claiming to the other children that Sheila had secretly obtained a cure for her venereal disease and was deliberately not telling her.

One day, Theresa became so angry about this that she hog-tied Sheila in a closet across from the back bedroom of the apartment as punishment for her deception.

Sheila had, in the eyes of her mother, given her venereal disease and then would not admit she had been cured of it. Theresa began to ration Sheila's food and refused to let her out of the closet.

At the end of May 1985, Theresa completely banned Sheila from being fed anything. She just remained crammed in that tiny closet next to the bathroom, which measured about two feet by two and a half feet—not big enough to keep a small dog in. Her feet were tied together with Ace bandages, her hands tied behind her back with white canvas wrist restraints bought at a medical supply store on Madison Avenue in Orangevale, near where they used to live. Theresa Knorr also removed the knob from the bathroom door and used it on the outside of the closet every time she wanted to open it to inspect her daughter. There was no handle inside the closet, so Sheila could not get out. Theresa Knorr told her daughter she would not feed her anything, even water, until she admitted what she had done.

"She wanted Sheila to confess," Terry has said. "That was mother's way. Beat them until they confess."

Weak from lack of food, stinking from perspiration in that steaming hot prison, Sheila knew there was only one way to survive. She confessed to her mother that, yes, she did have VD, and yes, she did get a cure. None of it was true, but Sheila only cared about one thing— getting out of that awful closet.

It was agony for Sheila as she crawled out of the tiny space that had been her home for more than a week.

Her first taste of freedom was probably as sweet for her as that of any escape from a POW camp.

Theresa Knorr once again switched to her caring, loving mother mode and gently helped her daughter drink some water. Sheila seemed to have made it against all the odds. Even the other children were surprised she had actually got out of the closet alive.

But Theresa Knorr was feeding her starving daughter water for an ulterior motive. She asked her what kind of drugs the doctor had given her when he administered the shot that cured her VD.

Sheila stumbled over her reply. That was enough for Theresa. She knew her daughter was lying. Within seconds Sheila was being dragged back to that closet from hell. Her freedom had been so brief. The black hole beckoned . . .

"PLEASE! PLEASE LET ME OUT OF HERE!"

The screams and moans coming from that closet soon became like audible wallpaper in the Knorr household. No one seemed to notice the sounds, but then Theresa Knorr had insisted on stuffing towels underneath the door to the closet so that it muffled her daughter's cries for help. No one seemed concerned about Sheila, except Terry, by now fourteen years of age.

She strained her ears to listen to any telltale signs of her sister's condition inside that small closet. A few days after she was locked in there for the second time, Terry heard Sheila rustling around, desperately peeling off her clothes because of the sweltering eighty-five degree heat that drifted through the day and much of the night.

The third day after Sheila's reincarceration, Terry waited until her mom went out on a rare trip to the local store before sneaking alongside the cupboard with some refreshment for her stifling, feverish sister. All she could find was two cans of beer.

She held a can to her sister's parched lips because her wrists were still bound behind her back. Sheila was sweating so profusely that her hair was wet through. She asked Terry for water, but at that moment Terry heard the sound of the Ford LTD returning. It was beer or nothing.

Sheila desperately swallowed it, much of the beer dribbled down the side of her mouth as she tried to drink the entire contents of one can in a single gulp. The alcohol might have helped deaden the pain just a little bit . . .

"There is a light above me. I think it's a hole. I'm gonna climb toward it."

Those were the last words Terry ever heard her sister Sheila utter. A few moments later she heard a thump, then another, then another . . . then silence.

Those muffled noises occurred as her sister tried to climb up the hard pine shelves inside the closet. Theresa Knorr had removed the lowest one so she could cram her daughter in there.

Sheila had been using the little ledges that the shelves sat on to hold them up, to climb up in the closet toward what she thought was the light of freedom. Those final sounds were the shelves crashing down on that emancipated girl.

For three more days Theresa Knorr and the rest of

her clan waited to hear if any more sounds came from that closet. They knew that an extended silence probably meant Sheila was dead. On the third day, June 21, 1985, Theresa Knorr sent Robert over by bicycle to get his brother Billy Bob from the apartment on Fulton he was sharing with Emily Lewis.

As soon as Billy Bob and Robert got back, Theresa grabbed the bathroom knob, slid it into the lock on the closet door and gingerly prized it open. Terry and Billy Bob stood by and looked on.

The awful stench that wafted out of the closet was followed by the inevitable proclamation by Theresa Knorr.

"She's dead."

Lying in that closet—barely large enough to store a box of books—was Sheila. Clotted blood was smeared crustily across her cheek. There was a puddle of blood on the floor in front of her face. Her torso was virtually naked. She was curled up in a fetal position with her arms behind her back.

"I can't recall whether her eyes were open or not, but I believe they might have been," said Terry years later, still haunted by the image of her sister's decaying corpse.

Theresa Knorr immediately suggested an outrageous plan to make sure that her daughter's death would never be linked to her family. She told the others she wanted to smash off Sheila's teeth with a hammer so that she could not be identified.

Moments later Theresa had second thoughts. She candidly confessed to the assembled children that even she considered the idea of smashing her own dead daughter's teeth to bits a little daunting.

Theresa then carefully peeled on a pair of yellow Playtex Living Gloves, ripped a plastic garbage bag up and used it to line the cardboard popcorn-cup box Billy Bob had brought home from his work at the nearby Century 21 movie theater on Howe Avenue. Theresa used that particular brand of gloves because they had a little diamond-shaped grip on them that obliterated all fingerprints.

Then Theresa sat on her bed with a stack of pink-and-blue-flowered pillowcases and slowly plucked all the hairs off those cases until there were none. She wanted to ensure her family had no connection to the body.

She then took the same pillowcases and lined the garbage bag inside the box with them to soak up any blood. Terry was then ordered to stand outside the house to make sure that nobody was nearby.

Inside, Billy Bob and Robert leaned into that tiny closet to pull their sister's remains out into the hallway. But the body would not move because half of the left side of Sheila's face was stuck to the floor where she had been frozen in death.

Billy Bob then decided to remove the door of the closet in order to get more access to take out the body. A few minutes later, having taken the door off, the brothers pulled at the rotting corpse and finally hauled it out.

The boys then put their sister's remains in the box— which had been so carefully prepared by Theresa Knorr —before wrapping silver duct tape around it. Then they carried the box outside and put Sheila in the trunk of their mother's Ford LTD. Next they packed shovels in the trunk. Robert got in the rear seat in the exact same spot where he sat when they took Suesan off to the mountains almost a year earlier.

Moments later Terry watched as her mom and two brothers drove off into the darkness to find a final resting place for Sheila.

This time Theresa made the long drive up Interstate 80 to the Highway 89 turnoff, but instead of driving to Squaw Valley where Suesan had been burnt, they found a new location near the runway at Truckee Airport.

Nine

> The battered child syndrome . . .
> characterizes a clinical condition in
> children who have received serious
> physical abuse, generally from a parent
> or foster parent.
>
> Pediatrician C. Henry Kempe, who
> invented the term "Battered Child
> Syndrome"

It was hardly surprising that Terry Knorr found herself choking back the urge to vomit as she started cleaning out that closet of death while her mother and brothers were out dumping Sheila's body in the mountains.

When they did eventually arrive home, her brother Robert cut the dismantled closet door up with a saw and then threw it in the Dumpster at the end of the driveway to the apartment complex that was attached to the house. Theresa and Billy Bob then collected all Sheila's belongings and dropped them in the same Dumpster. There was to be no olive oil burning ritual this time.

Terry, gasping against the pungent odor, tried to drink an iced grape Crush soda as she scrubbed away on her hands and knees inside that tiny closet. But all she could taste was death. She held her nose, swallowed hard and tried not to breathe in the acrid fumes.

Terry's brothers later told her they had tried to bury the box containing Sheila, but as they were digging, somebody had passed nearby and they got scared and drove off, leaving the container sitting in a clump of bushes.

Theresa Knorr had decided not to burn Sheila's body because she did not want it to look in any way similar to Suesan's death.

Terry's memories of her sister Sheila center around a cowboy hat that had become like a calling card for the pretty teenager.

"It was black velour or velvet and it had a big, like, feather decoration on the front. And she loved that hat. It was a personal belonging, I mean really personal."

Minutes after returning to the house, Theresa Knorr got rid of that hat. She thought that as long as any of her daughter's possessions were there, her spirit would still be there to haunt her.

Theresa Knorr also called up Wes Seegmiller, the lawyer who was chasing the insurance company for compensation after Sheila had been knocked down on Auburn Boulevard, and told him: "Forget it. I want you to drop the case."

Soon after Sheila's death, Theresa began voicing her hatred toward her daughter-in-law Connie Sanders.

She decided Connie's child should be taken away from her because she believed she was a bad mother. In order to do that, she figured she had to get Connie on unfit parent charges. With no evidence, she somehow became convinced Connie was drugging the baby so she did not have to feed it regularly.

Theresa decided that her youngest daughter, Terry, should become a police informant and help detectives set up Howard and Connie Sanders for a drug deal. First she told Terry to apply for a driver's license in her dead sister Suesan's name so that she could appear to be eighteen years old rather than fifteen. Then Terry could be recruited to make what police call a "controlled buy" of narcotics from her own brother and sister-in-law.

Local narcotics squad detective Richard Lauther had his suspicions right from the start when a mutual contact introduced him to "Suesan." The first disastrous drug purchase, in which "Suesan" was supposed to pick up some amphetamines from Howard Sanders, ended in a no-show. Detective Lauther dropped her a short time later, unaware of the brutality and death that allegedly had occurred inside the Knorr household, but highly suspicious of the young girl's real age.

When the detective had asked Terry about her sisters, she replied coolly: "One ran off with an Indian to go work in Canada, and my other sister just up and left home one day."

Terry was already passing into what psychiatrists describe as the denial stage of her horrendous childhood.

The Knorr's neighbor on Bellingham, Sean Martin, met up with Robert Knorr long after the family had moved to the small house just off Auburn Boulevard. Robert, unlike his younger sister, dropped a huge hint about what had happened to one sister, but not the other.

"It was weird," Martin later said. "First time I saw him, he said Sheila had met a used car salesman in Vegas who had swept her off her feet. Then a year later I met him and he told me that satan worshipers had come back and gotten his sister Suesan and set her on fire just off Highway 89."

On that second meeting with Sean Martin, Robert seemed to have changed a lot. He was a much more menacing character, and Sean warned his own brother Chris to steer clear of Robert as well. He seemed really strange. Almost dangerous.

One time, Sean actually visited the house just off Auburn Boulevard, but he could not get past the front door.

"I saw Robert in the street on his bike, and he persuaded me to take a spin down there. Well, it was so creepy at that house.

"As I walked up to the front door, I heard the mother beating Terry with a stick and I could hear other screams coming from the back of the house. Suddenly Robert freaked out completely and said I had to leave. 'My mom's freaking out' was all he would say. He was a very pale white color and seemed very shocked and upset."

After Theresa Knorr's plan to have her daughter-in-law arrested failed, she turned to Terry as the next object of her continuing war against the other women inside her family.

Those same handcuffs were pulled out of the closet and used on Terry with alarming regularity following the deaths of her sisters.

Theresa Knorr was consistent, if nothing else. She

had always punished the eldest daughter the most, followed by the second eldest and so on. But now there was only Terry left to bear the brunt of her mother's brutal regime.

In one horrendous incident, Terry claims the 250-pound Knorr jumped up and down on her while she was handcuffed underneath her antique oak desk. She crushed the young girl's stomach and seriously affected any chance of her ever having a child.

More than a year after Sheila's death—and following countless beatings at the hands of her mother—Terry heard the news that she hoped might just help to break up this incredibly unhappy family unit.

"We're outta here. We're movin' out," announced Theresa Knorr. "Terry, I gotta job for you . . ."

Ten

> "My mom was a criminal genius. She knew how to do things so she could get away with them. That's why I got the hell out."
> Terry Groves, in her statement to police

In the dense predawn mist, no one noticed the slight figure scrambling out of the back window of the small house just off Auburn Boulevard, the house that had been home to the Knorrs for the previous three years. The only noise was the occasional distant purr of a V8 engine on Interstate 80, a quarter of a mile to the west.

Terry Knorr's heart was beating at a furious rate. The seconds were ticking away. Terry would later recall how she had been instructed by her mother to burn their home to the ground. It was 3:40 A.M. on September 29, 1986.

Just a few hours earlier, Theresa Knorr had set out the plan in very professional terms. She had concluded that even though the closet where Sheila died had been very carefully cleaned and then another piece of board hammered over the top of the bloodstained floor, it still constituted a risk to her liberty. Lysol wouldn't work. Spic and Span would not get it out of the air. Fire had worked before on one of her daughters. Maybe it would

99

work again. Theresa Knorr was worried that whoever moved into the apartment after them would probably rip out that board and see the bloodstains.

She instructed her only surviving daughter to wear gloves, spray the Gulf charcoal lighter fluid all around the house quickly, then get out the window, before throwing the match in and running down the street to the motel where she was sharing a room with Robert.

The scared, confused sixteen-year-old spread the contents of the lighter fluid throughout the house and threw a lighted match on the floor *before* she had got out of the back window—and almost ended up suffering the same fate as her sister Suesan.

Scorching heat brushed the soles of her bare feet as she scrambled out of the window, the flames already licking through the back of the inside of the house.

Not daring to even look behind her, Terry just kept hearing her mother's orders: "Keep running. Keep running."

In the distance, sirens wailed.

As she weaved through the trailer park and toward the exit to Auburn Boulevard, Terry saw a fire truck turning in toward the house. But no one stopped her. No one even noticed her.

A few minutes later, out of breath and adrenaline still pumping furiously, Terry banged on the door of the room at the Las Robles Motel on Auburn. Theresa Knorr answered. Robert stood sheepishly in the background.

The fire at the house on the 2400 block of Auburn Boulevard was investigated by Officer Stan Brock. He found some clothes left in a rear bedroom by the Knorrs and rapidly came to the conclusion that there was absolutely no doubt the blaze had been started deliberately.

He also noted in his report on the day after the fire that Theresa "Knor Ross Sanders"—it should have been Knorr Cross Sanders—was three months behind with her rent and had been served with an eviction notice.

Case #86–86905 was never solved by the fire department, despite the fingers of accusation being pointed so firmly at Theresa Knorr and her clan. They tried to locate the family, but no one seemed to know where they had moved.

Howard Sanders thought he would actually behave like a dutiful son and go visit his mother a few days later, so he got quite a shock when he turned up at the house, completely unaware of what had happened.

Stunned by the burnt-out shell of the property, he strolled across the street to the property manager's office. But all that earned Howard was a very painful earache.

"You know what happened. Your family set fire to it!" the manager screamed hysterically.

"Well, do you know where they went?"

"No. Good riddance!"

She slammed the door so hard in his face he thought it would come off its hinges.

While no one had any clue as to the grisly killings that had allegedly occurred inside the house, there was a definite feeling in the neighborhood that Theresa and her brood of children were a strange bunch.

Susan Sullivan, who lived in the apartment block attached to the one-story house, witnessed firsthand a classic example of Theresa Knorr's cunning a few days after the blaze.

"She came up to my apartment and asked me if I had seen anyone hanging around outside the house, because some of her stuff was missing. I told her the door had been left wide open after the fire, so all sorts of people were coming and going. She seemed really pissed at me, almost as if she was accusing me of stealing stuff out of there. But from what I recall, there was nothing worth taking anyhow. It was all burnt to a crisp."

And she added: "I can't put my finger on it, but they were real weird people. The way they moved around. The way they talked. There was something not quite right about them. I wouldn't have wanted to cross them."

Fellow neighbor William Hall, who lived on the ground floor of the adjoining apartment block with his wife and young child and had become quite friendly with the Knorrs, has never forgotten that night. The heat was so intense, the walls of his apartment were too hot to touch. He believes he and his family were lucky to escape with their lives.

It wasn't as though Theresa Knorr had a split personality. She appeared to be aware of what she was doing and where she was. According to her surviving children, she did not suffer from blackouts or fits of fury. For Terry, it was a part of her life that she could not understand, except that her mother had exercised such control and power over her family that it appeared to drive her to committing acts of violence. Terry knew that whatever was inside her mother prevented her from truly loving anyone. Theresa Knorr had professed love to her children on many occasions, but she could not possibly have experienced true love. She never asked forgiveness. Terry believed that her only fear was that her precious boys would all eventually abandon her . . .

With Howard married and Billy Bob living with a girl on the other side of town, Robert became the apple of his mother's eye. He was the one person in her life whom she could cherish and adore. Yet there had been no strong ties between them when the killings began a few years earlier. Robert was the brother who turned squeamish at the sight of Suesan dying on the kitchen floor. He was also the one who sat terrified in the back of the car with her as she lay close to death en route to her outdoor cremation in the mountains.

Robert also took no direct part in actually pouring the gas over Suesan. Terry says it was Billy Bob who threw the match on her sister's fuel-soaked body.

After the fire at the house near Auburn Boulevard, Theresa Knorr and Robert stayed at the motel for a few days. Billy Bob was over at the apartment he shared with live-in lover Emily Lewis. Terry, meanwhile, saw the whole sequence of events as a perfect opportunity to escape, and she headed off for the red-light districts where Sheila had worked the streets just eighteen months earlier. Anything was preferable to life with her mother.

Eventually, Robert and his mother headed a couple of miles east to Carmichael, another suburb of Sacramento. It was around this time that she cut her long dark hair and started using a variety of blond wigs, and even sometimes dyed her hair as well. No one knows if her change in appearance was prompted by her own inbuilt fear of being one day apprehended for the alleged murder of her daughters, or just the simple vanity of an overweight woman reaching middle age.

But a blond and far more expensively dressed version of Theresa Knorr started to be seen out at the shopping malls in the area, usually with tall, handsome Robert dutifully following behind, loaded up with shopping bags.

Daughter-in-law Connie Sanders met Theresa Knorr at her apartment in Carmichael on one occasion. She was astonished by the new blond look. She also noticed that much of Theresa Knorr's anger and hatred seemed to have disappeared.

Theresa Knorr even persuaded Connie—once her sworn enemy—to try on the clothes she had worn when she was younger so she could see them once again. The fashion display by her daughter-in-law appears to have been a rather feeble attempt by a grossly overweight woman to fantasize about what might have been.

A few months later, Robert dropped by at his brother Howard's apartment, saying he wanted to see his niece and nephews.

Howard was naturally curious to find out how his mother was keeping. But Robert was mysteriously reticent.

"She's living with a guy," came the kid brother's reply. But he refused to say who or where.

"Is she planning on getting married to this guy or something?" Howard asked, well aware that his much married mother did not make a habit of living with men unless she intended to marry them.

Robert indicated that her intentions were to remarry, but he continued to refuse to provide any details of who might become Howard's latest stepfather.

Then his brother told him that their mother did not want Howard to know where she lived. The conversation ended abruptly, and Howard never saw his brother again.

Sometime later, Robert once again came looking for his older brother, but Howard had been jailed for a year for spousal abuse, so he never even realized his stepbrother was trying to find him.

By this time, Terry had already established herself in the same profession her tragic sisters had been involved in—prostitution. A brief reunion with her real father, Robert Knorr Sr., had ended abruptly when he tried to molest her after telling her that she reminded him of her mother Theresa.

Her passport to vice was, ironically, another California driver's license in the name of her dead sister Suesan Marline Knorr. This time the address given was 5804 Garibaldi Street, Sacramento. Unlike the earlier fraudulent license issued for Terry's undercover work on behalf of the narcs, this one described her hair as red and her weight as 155 pounds, an apparent increase of twenty-two pounds. At least the date of birth, 9–27–66, was the same.

The license had the words *Age 21 in 1987* emblazoned across it. But it provided Terry with a safe haven from child-care authorities who might put her in a home if she was picked up by cops and gave her true age at the time—just sixteen years old.

As Terry told detectives years later: "I got that so I could be with the older crowd and not be caught for being so young. The people I was living with at the time were basically hiding me out from my mother and my family."

Another license was eventually applied for by Terry so she could safely continue her work as a prostitute with a lady named "Debra." She convinced Terry to reapply for a license in Suesan's name the moment her sister would have been twenty-one so that she would not have problems going into local bars where many potential customers hung out.

Terry held on to that license and her sister's identity for another five years, in fear that her family or authorities might trace her.

Back on the mean streets of Sacramento's red-light district, word of Terry's tragic background filtered through to many of the girls working the area. Stories of abuse, sexual molestation, and poverty are two a penny among women and men forced to work in the vice trade. Some of Terry's new friends were particularly interested in adopting the identity of her other dead sister. One girl, known only as Mara, skimmed the details of Sheila's short life from conversations with Terry and got herself a driver's license in her name. It was years later that police realized the girl named as Sheila Gay Sanders on the license was in fact a petty criminal.

Terry's career on the streets was heavily influenced by Debra, who supplied her with drugs when she needed them and even owned a boutique in the area.

Debra was not exactly Terry's fairy godmother, but she did at least guide the teenager sufficiently to help her earn enough cash to stay out of her mother's clutches. She also introduced Terry to her lawyer, after Terry had told her about the killings of her two sisters.

Terry desperately wanted to see her mother brought to justice for those horrendous deaths. Up until that point, she simply had not met anyone in authority whom she could trust enough to even consider telling the full story to.

Debra provided her young friend with a Valium to swallow before her interview with the lawyer, to calm her nerves.

Terry told the lawyer the entire story, *but absolutely nothing happened.* There was no follow-up by him to her. He made no attempt to contact the police to get them to look into her claims. Terry was bewildered and decided that perhaps it had all been a stupid idea. She slotted those painful incidents back into a fragment of her memory bank and closed the door.

Unfortunately, Debra—who in a bizarre fashion had become almost like the mother Terry needed so desperately—eventually turned nasty on her young friend in just the sort of way Terry had become used to back in the Knorr household.

The incident that caused such an acrimonious parting

of the ways for the vice girl and her sugar mommy occurred when Terry tried to reverse Debra's car out of a
driveway, hit the gas pedal instead of the brake and
ended up crashing into a passing car.

A furious Debra threatened to make Terry work in a
notorious whorehouse in Vallejo to pay for the damage.
But Terry had no intention of being trapped in a vice
den.

Once again it was time for her to run away. Keeping
on the move somehow made her life more easy to cope
with.

Meanwhile, the lure of the bright lights of Reno just
a hundred miles east on Interstate 80 was proving irre-
sistible for Theresa Knorr and her son Robert. With a
few thousand dollars left over from the sale of the
house on Bellingham five years before, mother and son
decided to head to Nevada and the gambling halls of
Reno.

With her startling blond hairstyle in place, Theresa
thoroughly enjoyed spending hours at the slot machines
and card tables that adorn the ground floors of hotels
with such exquisite names as the Peppermill and the
Nugget. One of her favorite places was Fitzgerald's, a
name that would come to haunt her years later when
the hand of justice finally caught up with her.

Reno—the next biggest answer to Nevada's multibil-
lion dollar gambling habit after Las Vegas—is known in
some circles as "life's garbage can" because of the wan-
dering souls of northern and central California who
stream into the city from Interstate 80.

Theresa Knorr and Robert quickly put a deposit

down on a modest apartment on the 1200 block of West Second Street. But she must have found life as the matriarch to just one child a lot different from raising a brood of six.

Robert, nineteen, did not exactly feel indebted to his mother. Thanks to her, he had witnessed and, it is alleged, been forced to take part in, two appalling murders. Rather than cramp each other's style, they began living separate lives under the same roof. The control frenzy that seemed such an important part of Theresa Knorr's life was crumbling fast.

The streets of central Reno—with its neon and tatty skyscrapers—were a melting pot for young drifters, many of whom had run away from the sort of abusive homes that Robert and his brothers and sisters would have longed to be a part of, compared with the unspeakable horrors that allegedly occurred in their household.

Robert thrived unhealthily among the oddballs, and soon became caught up in Reno's lowlife. A charge of vagrancy followed after he was found asleep in a doorway to a store. A burglary was committed, and police later believed it was to obtain drugs.

Two Reno police officers called on Theresa's apartment looking for Robert one day. She was shaken by their visit. Her son's activities were alerting the authorities to her presence—and she wanted to avoid that at all costs. She got out a map, as do tens of thousands of Americans every day, and looked due east on her favorite Interstate 80. Salt Lake City, Utah, looked like the perfect place for her to start a completely new life . . .

* * *

Over at the office of Nevada County Sheriff William L. Heafey, detectives investigating the "Body in the Box" case as it had become known locally, believed they had a major breakthrough.

Fibers taken from the box appeared to match those of the interior carpet in the cab of long distance trucker Benjamin Herbert Boyle's vehicle. Boyle, from Potter County, Texas, had just been arrested on suspicion of a series of murders of upward of ten women. Detectives could not believe their luck after they sent off samples to Texas for examination and got the swift reply every law enforcement officer loves to hear: "It's your man."

Boyle told detectives he was also pretty grateful to have the opportunity to get the grisly murder off his chest. He was, as they say, singing like a canary.

In Nevada County the investigation into the "Body in the Box" case was closed.

It seemed that Theresa Knorr's awful alleged crimes were going to remain undetected. It emerged almost eight years later that the two samples of carpet from the serial-killing trucker's vehicle had actually come from the same place. A dreadful administrative error had somehow confused examiners in Texas into believing they had a sample of material from the cardboard box, when in fact the two pieces came from precisely the same truck.

Years later, one of the Placer County detectives investigating the crimes of Theresa Knorr tactfully described his neighboring county's error as a little embarrassing.

The biggest tragedy of all was that Theresa Knorr's

reign of terror could so easily have been brought to a close much sooner . . .

Meanwhile, inquiries into the identity of the other Jane Doe #4873/84—Suesan Knorr—continued to be made by the Placer County Sheriff's Department. At least that case was still marked open and unsolved.

On July 1, 1987, the FBI Academy at Quantico, Virginia—made famous partly thanks to the fictitious detective work of Agent Clarice Starling, played so convincingly by Jodie Foster in *The Silence of the Lambs*—contacted Investigator Brad Marenger at Placer County's substation at Tahoe City to assure him that the National Center for the Analysis of Violent Crime (NCAVC) and the Violent Criminal Apprehension Program (VICAP) had compared the crime analysis report submitted about Jane Doe #4858/84.

But, replied Quantico Unit Chief Alan E. Burgess, "no linkages have been detected at this time."

"Linkages" were what Investigator Marenger so desperately needed. He knew only too well that the chances of solving that particular murder were fading rapidly. It would take a miracle to even manage to identify her.

Eleven

The most important point about a
mother, your mother, is that she is your
mother for always.
Rachel Billington, Author

Salt Lake City's first real boom occurred when the
famous California Gold Rush of 1849–50 resulted in
large groups of emigrants trekking through the Salt
Lake Valley en route to California. One hundred forty
years later, Theresa Knorr made her own trek to the
city from the opposite direction, having decided to create a completely new life for herself.

The city itself, with its thriving cosmopolitan downtown area consisting of a quaint blend of modern tower
blocks and classic, older buildings, earned a glowing
tribute from *U.S. News & World Report*, which dubbed it
"an economic ace and one of sixteen newly bright stars
in the U.S. economic sky." With a population of
700,000 consisting of a multitude of backgrounds, it was
the perfect place for Theresa Knorr to blend into ano-
nymity.

While traveling east to Salt Lake, she passed the
hours away planning her new existence: a job, a home,
new friends, new surroundings, even a new name—she
decided to revert to her maiden name, Cross, and be-

came known as that from the moment she arrived in the city. It must have seemed terribly exciting to Theresa. The horrors she had inflicted back in Sacramento, according to her daughter Terry, must have been firmly slotted into a fragment of her mind she had no intention of reopening.

She even read up on the Mormons who founded Salt Lake City back in 1847 and had thrived ever since. U.S. soldiers were stationed in the area in the 1850s, bringing an immense amount of trade with them. Theresa Cross, as she was now known, was particularly interested in Mormon tradition. She had already decided that when the time was right, she would convert to the Church—it seemed the obvious thing to do if she were going to be easily and quickly accepted in the community.

Theresa Cross based herself in a modestly priced hotel near the downtown area, bought herself a copy of the Salt Lake City *Tribune* and the *Deseret News*, and started looking for a job. Her only previous employment had been as an orderly in convalescent hospitals, and she had already decided that looking after old ladies would be the perfect career for her new life. It also meant she would get free accommodation and free food and she would not have to live under the same roof as anyone prettier and younger than her.

Theresa's first job was as live-in help to seventy-two-year-old Alice Powell, riddled with multiple sclerosis, diabetes, and arthritis, and in serious need of twenty-four-hour attention. Alice's three daughters all interviewed Theresa in their sick mother's large, single-story home at 246 North Fourth East Street, Bountiful, a suburb just a few miles north of Salt Lake City. They immediately decided that Theresa was the perfect person for the job. Her transformation was under way.

Theresa Cross soon discovered that her new employer's family were worth many millions of dollars because Alice's parents had, at the turn of the century, bought vast lots of land in the area and then sold them during an economic boom in the fifties. Rumor had it that Alice was worth well over $4 million alone because her husband had retained some of the property and then cleverly developed his own share of the land before selling it.

Within weeks of Theresa starting her new job, Alice's relatives noticed a real improvement in the old lady's condition. They were particularly impressed by Theresa Cross's patience and good nature—something that none of her own children remember their mother for.

Alice Powell adored Theresa Cross. Theresa was very good to her and regularly took her on outings in her wheelchair. Theresa appeared to really care for the old lady's well-being, and the Powells were delighted with their new recruit.

Alice's sister-in-law, Fran Cheney, seventy-six, and husband Hal, seventy-eight, lived just a few miles north in another suburb, called Centerville, and took a real shining to Theresa.

The elderly couple spent many evenings at Alice's house in Bountiful talking to their newfound friend about the Mormon Church, which they both belonged to at the time. Theresa told them that she had been brought up a Catholic, but that part of her family was of Jewish descent. They spoke in great detail about the workings of the Bible. Theresa had referred to the Bible frequently when she shrieked excerpts from it at her children back in Sacramento.

Theresa Cross had a large collection of different Bibles and she knew the Old Testament particularly well. She regularly exchanged books with the Cheneys, and they gave her copies of a Christian Jewish newsletter about Orthodox Jews who accepted Christ. Eventually, Theresa Cross even joined the Church of Jesus Christ of Latter-day Saints, better known as the Mormons. Her transformation was complete.

But even though she went to the trouble to be baptized in the Church, she did not have much spare time to devote to it because she had to take care of Alice twenty-four hours a day.

During one evening with the Cheneys, Theresa gave a rare insight into her own upbringing. It was a story filled with rich detail and emotive visions of a childhood in the countryside. No one actually knows how much of it is fact and how much is fiction. She claimed she enjoyed a very happy life in the Midwest on a farm. She even talked aboout having owned a horse, and, she told the Cheneys, she was very fond of her father.

But then Theresa's voice lowered to a virtual whisper as she told Fran Cheney how her mother had died in her arms when she was just twelve years old, and she provoked even more sympathy by telling her two elderly companions that her grandmother died in the Holocaust.

But, Theresa Cross told her companions, she cursed God for taking her mother away from her at such an early age. She felt bitter about it and blamed that heartbreak for making her get married at a very young age. A few moments later she divulged her own secret guilt.

She told Fran and Hal she felt to blame for her mother's death and that God must have put a curse on her, and she said, "Don't ever go and die on your children."

Then Theresa surprised her two friends even further by telling them:

"I speak to my mother regularly through the spirits. Through seances and things like that. I still love her very much. When she died, we burned all her belongings on a fire."

That was exactly what, according to her daughter Terry, she did with tragic Suesan Knorr in that desolate countryside where they dumped her body.

Another weird aspect of that conversation with the Cheneys was that Theresa referred to her mother as if she were still alive.

But despite the obvious emotional turmoil she felt, Theresa Cross was very careful not to reveal the pain and anguish she had caused after she became a wife and a mother. Her conversations with the Cheneys suggest that perhaps she always believed that her mother was to blame for everything.

Theresa's lapses revealed small fragments of her past. Like the time she told Fran and Hal about her cruel husband. She never disclosed which one. She never even admitted she had been married more than once.

But Theresa Cross did tell Fran and Hal she believed her husband was a satanist.

However, Theresa told her friends: "I wouldn't want

to put anyone through what I suffered. I couldn't tell you the things he made me do."

Then Theresa simply changed the subject. Fran knew not to pry any further into her background.

One day, Theresa took her sick and elderly patient Alice to Park City, Utah, more than thirty miles away, for a special outing. The Cheneys were most impressed when they heard that Theresa had paid for a three-course lunch for the old lady in the ski resort, with her own money.

Fran and Hal Cheney were concerned that their new friend was overworking herself. During her first eighteen months at Alice's house in Bountiful, Theresa Cross never once took a vacation.

"We were so worried about Theresa. Looking after an old lady is relentless work, and if you don't take any time off, it wears you down after a while," said Fran.

In fact, Theresa was saving up her $1600 monthly salary and planning her next move with military precision. She had already bought herself a Dodge in her favorite bright red color to get around in. Her new life had given her new energy—and a determination to further her career in geriatric care.

In the spring of 1990, Theresa Cross enrolled in a night school at the Holladay Health Care Center, about fifteen miles southeast of Salt Lake City, in an attempt to qualify as a fully trained nurses' aide in general health care.

On her first night at the imposing three-story building in Holladay, she met classmate Keith Bendixen. The sixty-seven-year-old hospital orderly was immediately impressed by Theresa, whom he considered to be a classy lady.

At first Keith—who worked in the day at the same health-care center in the Salt Lake Valley where the night school was held—felt too shy to exchange anything more than mere pleasantries with the striking but heavy-looking woman. But at break times from the grueling eight-hour weekly class, the two would walk to the soda machine down the hallway together, and they gradually started to strike up conversations.

To begin with, Theresa talked virtually nonstop to Keith about geriatric care and told him how she looked after an old lady in Bountiful. She even spun a yarn about having one time lived up near Idaho Falls where she did some nursing.

She never once mentioned Sacramento.

It seemed to Keith as if she was deliberately talking mainly about work so as to avoid any pointed questions about her personal life. But then, the course was incredibly hard work, and anyone who could work from 4:00 P.M. to midnight at night school had to be very dedicated.

About a month into the course, the classmates all had to work three eight-hour days in the actual care center as part of the practical side of their training. Theresa impressed everyone with her intelligence and devotion to the job.

She had a long list of duties that had to be carefully checked off, and most of the nurses ordering her around were younger and, in many cases, prettier. Theresa Cross was particularly caring toward a number of old ladies with broken hips who had been moved to the health-care center from hospitals where their beds were needed for more urgent cases.

"She would get those old ladies up, get 'em dressed, comb their hair and shave them. Then put them in a wheelchair and take 'em to the dining room. Then she would feed 'em, take 'em out of the dining room, and put 'em back to bed. She also had to toilet 'em at least several times a day, as well as clean their bed and put fresh sheets on," explained Keith admiringly.

Every week the class of ten was given a progress test. Theresa passed with flying colors each and every time. Keith said she was always immaculately dressed and she talked with a very nice accent.

"In class she was always putting her hand up to answer questions and the teacher was always saying she did real good in everything."

At the end of the three-month course—which cost just eighty dollars—Theresa sailed through the big end-of-term exam and became fully qualified as a nurses' aide in general health care.

A few months after finishing the course, Theresa called Keith Bendixen up and asked him if either he or anyone in his family would like to earn some extra money by relieving her for the occasional day at Alice Powell's home in Bountiful.

Soon he, his wife, and daughter Marcella were all taking turns to stand in for Theresa whenever she needed days off. She never explained where she was going.

On one occasion, Keith says he stayed overnight at the house after Theresa came home late from some assignation or other. Keith helped fix the hydraulic lift that was used to get Alice into the bath. But the next day, one of Alice's sisters told Theresa they did not want a man staying overnight in the house. Keith never stayed there again. But he did work at the house at least twenty more times.

Often, Theresa would take Keith and his wife out with her and Alice for a meal at the Seven Seas Japanese restaurant in the shopping mall near the house. Sometimes they would also eat out at the Red Lion Cafe. As usual, Theresa showed great generosity by always treating everyone.

Keith received his wages for helping look after Alice Powell out of the $1600 a month that Theresa was paid. Theresa also shelled out cash for most of the delicious food she prepared at the house, because her housekeeping allowance from Alice's daughters of $250 a month did not cover everything.

Keith loaned her countless books on nursing care, and she loaned him her math and chemistry books. She also owned dozens of books on the development of certain drugs.

Keith remembers Theresa's cooking as being superb. He would always say a blessing before each meal, which Theresa seemed impressed by.

"Bless this food and do our bodies good and help us. Amen."

One time, Theresa told Keith she had been on a trip down to San Diego to see her son. It was a rare reference to her family, and untrue, since she had no son in southern California.

But even more significantly, Theresa Cross told Keith

she had just one other son and he had died in a motor-cycle crash. *She did not mention her three daughters.*

Sometimes Keith, his daughter Marcella, and Theresa would do some Bible readings together. And at breakfast Theresa would sit buried in her chemistry books once Alice had sat down to eat. She told Keith that she was studying hard in the hope of one day being allowed to enroll for a full four-year nursing course to get an R.N. degree. Theresa Cross was thinking big-time. Her life had taken on an entirely new dimension.

Once again Theresa talked in fictional terms about her upbringing; this time she claimed she had been raised in places like Kentucky and Tennessee. She admitted she wasn't close to her family but had written to them on occasions. Keith—who had at one time sold cars and real estate in California—was intrigued by his new friend. But there was something about her . . . he just could not quite put his finger on it.

In Sacramento, more Knorr family problems were brewing following a surprise visit to Billy Bob's cozy home in North Highlands, near Sacramento, by way-ward brother Robert.

At first Billy Bob was fairly pleased to see his kid brother. It had been at least four years since he and Theresa Knorr had skipped town for Reno, and he'd thought about them both many times.

But when Robert's brief visit turned into months, Billy Bob started to notice habits of his brother's that he never knew existed.

Robert was always out until late, and waking up Billy Bob when he struggled into the apartment in the early hours. And Robert was behaving "differently" from what he had been like before.

Ultimately, Billy Bob kicked Robert out of the house, and never saw him again.

Billy Bob was very careful not to introduce his brother to his new pretty blond girlfriend DeLois, whom he had met when the two attended a radio broadcasting school in Sacramento. They were already deeply in love and talking about marriage.

Twelve

> The single most consistent finding
> regarding juvenile homicide is that kids
> who kill, especially those who kill
> family members, generally have
> witnessed or have been directly
> victimized by domestic violence.
> Charles Patrick Ewing, author

When bartender Robert Ward walked into work for the night shift at Red's Place on North Nellis Boulevard, in Las Vegas, on November 7, 1991, he could not have had any idea that he was about to become the next victim of the Knorr family's sick and twisted household.

For Robert Knorr, life in Vegas had become a game of desperate stakes since arriving from Reno. He had no money and was living on the streets or scrounging a bed for the night from some passing stranger. Reno might have been the garbage can of northern and central California, but Vegas seemed to be the waste disposal unit for the entire country.

And Robert's earlier split with his mom when they were both up in Reno was probably the final straw as far as his own sense of self-preservation was concerned. Ironically, while he may well have been desperate to get away from her, she did in many ways protect him from himself. How could a man barely out of his teens have any sense of moral purpose in life after experiencing and, his sister Terry claims, taking part in the killing of his two sisters?

Throughout his short life, Robert Knorr had demonstrated an escalating propensity toward violence, an important trait of an emerging murderer. As a child he had witnessed such horrors that he later admitted he had no real control over his temper. In some ways, he was just asking for the intervention of the criminal justice system. He barely recognized society's laws because punishment had no real meaning to him—he had just been through a childhood that no human being should ever have to endure.

By the time Robert Knorr found himself hanging around outside Red's Place that warm evening, casing the joint and planning an armed holdup, he had all but given up on life as we know it.

Ten minutes later, bartender Robert Ward was dead after Knorr held him up with a pistol in yet another desperate attempt to feed his drug habit. The police picked Knorr up without a struggle a couple of blocks from the bar a few minutes later.

Intriguingly, Robert Knorr did not even bother to ask for a lawyer when police took him down to the local precinct to be booked and thrown in a holding cell. His only request was for them to get in touch with his mother. He gave them an address. But when detectives contacted Theresa Knorr, she never returned their calls. The son who must have been turned into a killer by those awful scenes at that little house off Auburn Boulevard, was being snubbed by the very person who created his downfall.

Las Vegas police pressed for first-degree murder charges, and with it, the potential of a cell on Nevada's death row. But in the end they reduced the charge to second-degree murder in exchange for his admission of guilt.

On June 25, 1993, he stood before the Eighth Judicial District Court in Las Vegas and was sentenced to sixteen years. His mother never did bother to contact him.

But Robert's problems were of no concern to Theresa Cross, as she was now known. In Salt Lake City, she did not even acknowledge the existence of a son in Las Vegas. She had a new life, after all.

However, there was a slight hiccup to her plans when she took a one-month vacation from her job at Alice Powell's place in Bountiful and ended up staying away for eight weeks. Once again she used that now familiar tale of going to visit her son in San Diego. No one knows where she really went.

Not surprisingly, Alice's daughters decided that they needed someone a little more reliable in charge of their mother, and Theresa was dismissed for taking the extra time off without permission. (Alice's daughters insist to this day that she walked out on the job.)

Ann Cristofersen, fifty-six, took over from Theresa at the Powell house in Bountiful, and she completely discounts reports of her predecessor's diligence.

"I believe that she left Alice alone on many occasions. Neighbors have told me they would often call around and discover that Theresa was out and Alice was here by herself."

However, Ann Cristofersen made much more serious allegations about Theresa Cross's treatment of Alice Powell, who is basically unable to attend to anything for herself:

"I think she was sometimes physical with Alice. I have no doubt that she slapped her a few times and used to leave her on the toilet for hours. When I arrived here, I had to spend months getting Alice's confidence because she was so scared every time she had to be taken to the toilet."

If Ann Cristofersen's claims have any real substance, they completely contradict the opinion of many others in Salt Lake City.

But Theresa's falling out with the Powell family had no effect whatsoever on her friendship with Fran and Hal Cheney over at Centerville. In fact, the elderly couple took pity on Theresa when they heard she was no longer working for Fran's sister-in-law and offered to let her stay in their house while they were away on a trip to Russia in 1992.

Theresa kept the red-brick, detached two-story house built in the 1920s spotless, watered all the plants, and behaved like the perfect guest while they were on their travels. For Theresa Cross, the Cheneys' hospitality would remain indented on her conscience. She never forgot their kindness.

But for the time being she needed to find another job as a home help to an elderly person. Once again she picked up the local newspaper, the *Deseret News,* and studied the jobs columns in the classified section.

* * *

Less than ten miles away from where Theresa Knorr was reading that newspaper, her wayward daughter, the only surviving female child in the Knorr family household, was getting married to the man she hoped would help wipe out those awful memories forever.

In an extraordinary twist of fate, both mother and daughter had ended up running away to the same city. Incredible though it may seem, neither of them apparently had any clue as to each other's whereabouts.

Terry had escaped from the evil clutches of vice girl Debra and then another even more unpleasant madam in Sacramento, when she met and fell in love with softly spoken, hardworking Mike Groves.

He had proclaimed his love for Terry virtually from the moment he clapped eyes on her in a bar, and the two had decided to elope back to Mike's home in Salt Lake City to get married, settle down, and live happily ever after. But fairy tales never come true . . . especially if you come from a family like the Knorrs.

Terry had so many reasons to want to leave those streets of Sacramento: her mother's abuse, the murders of her two sisters, the sexual molestation, the prostitution, the drugs. Anywhere had to be better than Sacramento as far as she was concerned.

So when she and Mike traveled up to Salt Lake City, Terry—just like her mom had done a couple of years earlier—saw the streets of this thriving city paved in the sort of happiness she had never experienced in her entire life.

The marriage ceremony was a modest affair held at

Mike's parents' house in Sandy, a suburb eight miles southeast of Salt Lake City.

Matron of honor Heidi Sorenson, who went on to become Terry's best friend, explained: "It was a small, friendly gathering. A simple champagne toast after the ceremony. But I remember that Terry seemed so genuinely happy to be getting married. It was as if she had at last found some true happiness."

The couple could not afford a honeymoon, but that did not matter to Terry. She had Mike and a new life—that was all that mattered.

But within months of marrying Mike Groves, all that pain and anguish was to return. The main problem up in Salt Lake City was that she was sharing her in-laws' huge, badly maintained house, in the relatively wealthy suburb of Sandy. And besides being home to Ma and Pa, there was also Mike's big, slow-witted brother to contend with. The house was dark, gloomy, filled with cheap, broken, outdated furnishings and filthy carpet on the floor. The Groves had bought it more than thirty years earlier, and a local housing boom had turned the once deserted area into an upper-middle-class neighborhood.

The parents tried hard initially. They made sure that Terry and Mike got some privacy in their basement apartment attached to the main house only by a spiral staircase into the ground floor hallway. But what Terry did not realize until she got to Sandy was that everyone in the house drank. Soon, domestic arguments were commonplace, and although not on anything like the scale of Sacramento, they had the effect of reminding Terry over and over again of her horrendous childhood.

However much she tried, she could not stop herself from getting drawn into these increasingly violent rows between Ma, Pa, and Mike. She had to act to stop the arguments before something dreadful happened. Subconsciously, she felt partly to blame. She felt she was the catalyst for yet more domestic upheaval. Eventually it got to her. She had a fight with Mike, hit him, and the police charged her with assault.

Terry soon became a familiar face at the Salt Lake County Jail, where she would spend many nights cooling off after yet another flare-up at home. Terry got quite aggressive inside prison and was known to certain prison officers as a hot-tempered troublemaker.

Sandy Police Department patrolman David Lundberg rolled up to the house in his all-white SPD Taurus one time in 1991. Although police did not arrest anyone on that occasion, Lundberg vividly recalled the house because it was such a high-income home maintained at a low income.

He recalled: "They were all fighting like cats and dogs. I tried to defuse the situation as best I could, but it all seemed so dysfunctional. In the end we settled things down, but it was pretty obvious there would continue to be problems there."

David Lundberg never forgot his visit to the house in Sandy, and it would hold him in very high stead one day a couple of years later.

Still only in her early twenties, Terry's desperate search for a happy life had seemingly ground to a complete halt. She loved her husband very much, but she feared that her mother's evil ways were manifesting themselves inside her now.

Wed at a young age. No money. Constant rowing. Her married life was turning into a mirror image of the woman whom she so hated and despised.

If Terry had realized that her own mother—the very woman whom she claims caused all her problems—was living a relatively charmed existence just a few miles away, would it have made any difference? As it was, Terry's difficult marriage incited her to try once again to do something to bring her mother to justice. She believed that the only way to finally destroy Theresa Knorr's appalling influence was to get someone to believe her incredible story of life inside that horrendous family.

For the next few months she desperately tried to find someone to tell her story to. First she told a friend, Rhonda Morris, who sat and listened intently to Terry but then decided to ignore her extraordinary claims because she thought Terry had said her mother was already in jail for the killings.

Terry went on to inform at least five other individuals about the murders, including a psychiatrist in Salt Lake City, two employees at the Valley Mental Health Clinic, and even a mental health counselor she encountered during one of her spells inside the Salt Lake County Jail.

But no one seemed concerned enough to actually go to the police themselves. Many of them could not accept or believe Terry's story of mental, physical, and sexual torture.

Meanwhile the domestic crisis inside her in-laws' house in Sandy continued. When would someone stand up and take notice of what she was saying?

Thirteen

The vast majority of abused children
treat their parents much better than
their parents have ever treated them.
Paul Mones, *When a Child Kills*

Terry felt an icy chill run through her body. She shivered, looked up. It was pitch-black, except for a tiny sliver of light in the corner above her. Instinctively, she pushed the palm of her hand upward. It smacked against something cold and plastic. She pushed hard again, this time with both hands. She had to get to that light. It was her only chance. But the ceiling would not move. The only noise was the crisp crumpling of the frozen bags that lined the floor she was lying on. As she adjusted her position, her elbow brushed the side of the wall next to her. It gave off a slight burning sensation because of the subzero temperatures. Terry was trapped in a deep freezer.

Sitting on the door to the coffin-shaped icebox was her 250-pound mother. She was punishing her youngest daughter because she thought Terry had been saying bad things about her to her teacher at school.

Inside the freezer, Terry gasped for air. Clouds of icy steam surrounded her every breath. She looked up at that small crack of light once again.

"There's a light above me. I think it's a hole. I'm gonna climb toward it."

"There's a light above me. I think it's a hole. I'm gonna climb toward it."

Terry's sister's voice just would not stop repeating the words over and over again.

Just then a movement from above. The door opened. The bulky shape of her huge mother was silhouetted against the light. Unlike her tragic sister Sheila, Terry had made it to that light above.

Terry awoke from her nightmare relieved to find that this time it had all been a fantasy. The freezer incident had been yet another appalling act committed against her by her mother a few years earlier. Her dreadful dreams had haunted her for more years than she cared to remember and they left her feeling angry, confused, even betrayed. Her anger was because her mother had disappeared into thin air and allegedly got away with murder. She felt confused because Theresa Knorr's liberty implied that it was okay for parents to abuse and hate children—maybe they all did that? But the worst aspect was the betrayal that Terry felt because none of the people she told about her terrible childhood experiences had done anything to help bring Theresa Knorr to justice.

Only a few days earlier, Alan Rice, a counselor at the Valley Mental Health Center in Salt Lake City, had pleaded with Terry to go and tell the police one last time after he listened with horror to her story. But no one understood that Terry was afraid of walking into a police station alone and retelling her story. In any case, it had got to the point where she wondered if it was worth it.

But that evening—with Alan Rice's advice still ringing in her ears—Terry decided to pour out her innermost secrets to Heidi Sorenson, her best friend in Salt Lake City.

They had become very good friends after Terry married Mike Groves, who just happened to be Heidi's then-husband's best pal. Heidi was the matron of honor at the wedding ceremony held at Terry's in-laws' house in Sandy. Terry would often drive over to Heidi's place in her little truck, where she would sit and chat with her friend and maybe cook up a little pasta.

Heidi, now twenty-six, explained: "Terry seemed to be very introverted. Into herself. I remember when I first met her she was very difficult to get to know. She is a jeans and T-shirt type of person and comes across as kinda hard-core because of what she has been through."

Heidi and Terry were sitting around at Heidi's neat duplex home in Woods Cross, yet another Salt Lake City suburb, on June 26, 1990, when Terry told her friend she had something on her mind.

"I've got these things that are really bothering me. D'you mind if I tell you 'bout them?" asked Terry hesitantly. She was close to giving up on ever getting her mother brought to justice, but she felt the urge to have a sounding board, a shoulder to cry on, and Heidi seemed the only true, genuine friend she had.

Heidi had absolutely no clue what Terry was about to tell her. Terry had never even told her husband the full details of those horrendous years in the Knorr household, and it was hardly something you talked about over popcorn at the movies or dinner at Denny's, which were the sort of things the two couples had done together.

Tears welled up in Terry's eyes before she had even begun to tell her friend. Heidi's two young children were still up, but playing so noisily in the kitchen that they would never have overheard the disturbing story Terry was about to reveal.

She told Heidi everything: the killings of her sisters, the beatings and torture she received, the abuse inflicted to and by her brothers, her sister's mottled hair when they found her body rotting in that closet, Suesan's desperate cries for help.

Terry then lowered her voice to a whisper.

"Sometimes I think I am going crazy. I wonder if I imagined it all. No one ever seems to believe me."

Heidi was so stunned by her friend's account of life as a child that for a few moments she also wondered if Terry was actually telling the truth.

"It was so bizarre. It was hard to believe things like that could have happened," says Heidi now.

Then she felt a chill in the air, thinking about what her friend had just told her.

"The house seemed to get real cold after she told me. It was weird. Almost as if . . ."

Heidi put her arm around Terry, who sobbed: "I can't understand why nothing has been done. I can't understand."

Heidi was appalled by what Terry told her. "It just wasn't right that someone could get away with doing those things," she said.

Terry had so much bottled up inside her, but she felt she could trust Heidi. She told her friend about the never-ending nightmares and how what had happened had stopped her from getting into many relationships. How it had affected her schoolwork; she did not even graduate from school.

Heidi particularly remembered that because the two women were, in many ways, like chalk and cheese. She had been to college and was even studying nights at business school to get more knowledge of the legal aspects of big businesses.

It was around 9:00 P.M. by the time a tearful Terry finished telling her horror story. Heidi, appalled by what she had heard, felt she had to help in some way. Then she remembered that her sister used to go out with the son of the local sheriff. He would do something, she thought. But when Heidi told Terry that she was going to call Sheriff Clarence Montgomery of the Woods Cross Sheriff's Department immediately, Terry was not overly impressed. After all, she had already told a number of people she thought were in authority, and they had done absolutely nothing.

But this is a cop, Heidi assured her. Not some fancy psychiatrist or social worker. This was someone out on the streets who would actually know how to get some action. She picked up the phone.

"I got someone here you gotta talk to, Sheriff. I need you to come over tonight . . ."

The moment Heidi mentioned the word "murder," Montgomery's ears pricked up. Woods Cross, a suburb with a population of just 6,000, ten miles north of Salt

Lake City, had seen only one murder in more than thirty years.

"I'll be right over."

By 11:00 P.M. Sheriff Clarence Montgomery was sitting down on Heidi's couch, his Sony Dictaphone minicassette recorder whirling as he prepared to listen to the most extraordinary account of domestic abuse he would ever hear, even in his long and distinguished career.

With the kids now safely tucked up in bed, a deathly, expectant silence shrouded the house. Sheriff Montgomery asked red-eyed young Terry sitting opposite him to run through the whole story one more time.

Terry started from the beginning once again. Maybe this time something would actually get done. Heidi sat next to her friend, holding her hand for comfort.

Heidi was surprised to notice Sheriff Montgomery's attention wavering several times as Terry told her account of life back in Sacramento. In fact he dozed off several times. But it was very late at night.

At around 12:30 P.M. the minicassette clicked off as it came to the end of the second side of the tape—and that marked the end of the interview. Unfortunately, the batteries in the machine were too low to record the latter half of the interview, it was later revealed by embarrassed investigators. Heidi did not dare tell Terry that she was a little concerned about the sheriff's catnapping. She just hoped that something would now be done to track down Theresa Knorr.

Terry went to great efforts to emphasize to the sheriff that she had told many others, who had done nothing, and she hoped some action would be taken. The sheriff assured her that it would.

Next day, Montgomery carefully wrote up a report of his visit to Heidi Sorenson's home. Then a letter from Woods Cross Chief of Police Paul Howard was enclosed with Montgomery's report, plus the tapes of the interview, and dispatched to the Sacramento Police Department's Homicide Division Commander.

The letter read:

Dear Investigator,

Theresa Knorr Groves of 2020 E. Pepperwood Drive, Sandy, Utah, contacted one of our officers and related some information concerning a possible homicide that occurred in 1982 and a second homicide that occurred in 1985 or 1986 in your area.

Theresa Groves, DOB 8/5/70, stated that she was raised in the Sacramento area and lived with her mother, Theresa J. Knorr, possible date of birth 3/14/46. Her maiden name was Theresa Cross, but she has used the names of Boyington, Sanders, Harris, Knorr, and Cross. She has worked as a nurse.

She lists the children as Howard, DOB 7/16/63; Sheila, DOB 3/13/65; Susan [sic], DOB 9/27/66; William, DOB 9/17/67; Robert, DOB 12/31/68; and herself.

She says that her mother tortured and shot Susan [sic], and then disposed of her body in a car fire after several months. This occurred in 1982.

Her mother also killed Sheila by physically abusing her, keeping her tied up in a closet, and after she died the body was disposed of by a car fire near Truckee.

Her mother had also shot her first husband but had been acquitted of that homicide.

These incidents occurred at 2410 Ivory Boulevard, Apt. #A, but the apartment had been burned down to cover up the evidence of Sheila's death.

Being fearful for her life, Theresa left the Sacramento area and has been in the Salt Lake area since 1988. She has recently been arrested for intoxication and has used drugs in the past and is currently seeing an Alan Rice at the Valley Mental Health Center in Salt Lake. She told him about this information and he advised her to give the same information to the police.

She is currently living within the jurisdiction of the Sandy City, Utah, Police Department and was only in our area to visit a friend at the time she contacted our officer.

I have run the names NCIC with negative results on any of them.

Our officer did record the majority of the conversation, however, without his realizing it, the batteries went dead and the entire conversation was not recorded. I have enclosed the tape for your use.

If we can be of any further assistance, please contact me.

Sincerely,

Paul Howard
Chief of Police

In Sacramento, Howard's letter, Montgomery's report and tape—sealed in a registered envelope—were received by Lt. Ken Walker, head of the homicide detail. He assigned a detective to look into the allegations. That detective checked the details out and promptly proclaimed the allegations an unlikely tale after failing to link any homicides with Terry's claims about the deaths of her sisters.

While there certainly are a number of errors in the letter, the basic essence of what had occurred is clearly and accurately stated.

Terry's phone number is at the beginning of the letter, yet no one from Sacramento ever called her.

Unfortunately, as it later emerged, the police only contacted officials in Nevada County, where the body of Sheila had been incorrectly linked to the killings committed by Texan truck driver Benjamin Herbert Boyle. Sacramento detectives never contacted the Placer County Sheriff's Department, where Suesan's charred remains were discovered and her murder continued to be unsolved. Years later, as questions flew around the Sacramento police headquarters, officials noted that Terry had, in her statement to Montgomery, mentioned Truckee as the location where Suesan's body was burned, and they presumed that to be in the Nevada County jurisdiction.

When the calls from Woods Cross Sheriff's Department stopped coming in after those first few weeks of activity, Terry assumed that yet again her pleas for justice had gone unnoticed. Perhaps it would be better to stop retelling those horror stories and get on with her life, she thought to herself. But the nightmares just would not let her forget.

Heidi and Terry never mentioned it ever again. In fact the two friends lost touch when Heidi's marriage fell apart and Terry's seemed under severe stress.

Heidi is still astonished by the lack of a police investigation following Sheriff Montgomery's visit to her home that night.

Those vivid images of child abuse retold so chillingly by Terry haunted her friend Heidi for years. It got so bad at one stage that she could not bring herself to go out to the storage shed in her backyard because it reminded her of the closet where Sheila had perished.

Heidi could even imagine the smell of rotting flesh inside that closet, thanks to an incident years earlier when she found herself standing near a corpse in a hospital elevator.

"There was no light in there and I remember getting goose bumps when I went in it. I couldn't stop thinking about what happened," recalled Heidi.

Just ten miles south of Woods Cross, Theresa Cross, as she now called herself, was blissfully unaware of just how close she had come to being arrested. Her main priority at that time was finding a new job following her departure from Alice Powell's house in Bountiful.

As she carefully studied the classified section of the *Deseret News,* an advertisement caught her eye.

Care Giver for elderly lady. Full time salary plus room and board. Please phone . . .

A few hours after calling the number, Theresa Cross —the one-time alleged mom from hell turned saintly nurse to the sick and elderly—was handing over two sparkling references to retired bank executive Bud Sullivan and his sister Pat Thatcher, who were interviewing her for the job of care giver to their elderly mother, Alice Sullivan.

Bud Sullivan was particularly impressed by her knowledge of medications. Pat, whose husband Vere was a retired Salt Lake City detective, was just as enthusiastic.

Theresa Cross was particularly proud of her certificate from the state government that proclaimed her to be a fully qualified health care worker. She even gave Bud Sullivan the number of her certificate just in case he wanted to check it out.

"I figured that since she gave me the number, it had to be true," remembered Bud.

By the time Theresa Cross had left Bud's mom's home in east Salt Lake City where the interview was conducted, both he and his sister were convinced she was the perfect person for the job.

Bud had actually hired another woman a few days earlier, but she had not even showed up for her first day of work at the Sullivan house.

"Theresa seemed so solid in comparison. We both knew she was the right one for the job," said Bud.

Fourteen

The emotional development of children
is intimately connected to the safety
and nurturance provided by their
environment.
Bessel Van Der Kolk,
Harvard Medical School psychiatrist

By December of 1992, Theresa Cross was lapping up her new life in Salt Lake City with relish. All those memories of what happened back in Sacramento had been neatly filed away. She was now the loving, caring nurse to elderly Alice Sullivan, and the added bonus was Alice's family, who all readily accepted Theresa Cross into their lives and homes. Later, they used words like "good" and "kind" to describe the woman whom her daughter Terry claims is one of the most cold-blooded mothers in criminal history.

"Theresa was a great person. My mother just loved her. Everybody in the family loved her," recalled Bud Sullivan, Alice's son.

That affection toward Theresa Cross came to a pleasant head at Christmastime that year. Bud and his sister Pat insisted that she be involved in every aspect of the yuletide festivities. The contrast between the punishments she inflicted so horrifically on her children that

Head bowed, William Knorr appeared at the Placer County Court House in February of 1994. He never once looked in the direction of his mother. Attorneys claimed he was devastated by his arrest and the subsequent charges. (WENSLEY CLARKSON)

Theresa Knorr and her son William together for the first time in years during that same appearance at the Placer County Court House. Knorr never once looked her son in the eye. (WENSLEY CLARKSON)

William Knorr in a
police photograph
taken shortly after his
arrest for murder.
(PLACER COUNTY POLICE)

Robert Knorr in a
photograph taken
following his
conviction for
murdering a bartender
in Reno, Nevada.
(PLACER COUNTY POLICE)

Sandy Police Detective David Lundberg, who played an important role in persuading Terry to bring her mother to justice. He later admitted to acting as Terry's agent when she secured a lucrative television movie deal with a Hollywood producer.
(WENSLEY CLARKSON)

Detective Johnnie Smith, who headed the Placer County task force that eventually traced Theresa to Salt Lake City. By coincidence, he was also one of the officers involved in the murder investigation into the death of Theresa Knorr's sister, Rosemary Norris.
(WENSLEY CLARKSON)

Tahoe City Detective Sergeant John Fitzgerald at the location in Squaw Valley where the burnt remains of Suesan Knorr were discovered in 1984. Fitzgerald and Johnnie Smith personally detained Theresa Knorr in Salt Lake City.
(WENSLEY CLARKSON)

Terry Knorr's best friend, Heidi Sorenson, at her Salt Lake City duplex where Terry poured her heart out about the deaths of her two sisters. She later made a statement to local investigators who failed to act on her information. (WENSLEY CLARKSON)

Terry Knorr, close to tears following the arrest of her mother, during a Salt Lake City KUTV news segment that revealed the extraordinary story surrounding the deaths of her two sisters. (KUTV)

The house on Bellingham Way in Sacramento, where Theresa Knorr and her family lived before the deaths of her daughters. The alleged initial shooting of Suesan, which left her seriously injured with a bullet lodged in her back, occurred in this house just before they moved to the house on Auburn Boulevard. (WENSLEY CLARKSON)

The small, single-story house in Sacramento where Suesan Knorr was allegedly starved following her earlier shooting. According to Terry Knorr, less than a year later, her other sister Sheila died after being locked in a small closet following a series of horrific abuse. (WENSLEY CLARKSON)

The railroad track where the body of Theresa Knorr's sister, Rosemary Norris, was discovered under suspicious circumstances. Investigators later concluded that Knorr did not play any part in her sister's murder, although they spent many weeks looking into links between her and her sister's husband. (WENSLEY CLARKSON)

Howard Sanders as a baby in the kitchen sink just yards from where his mother, Theresa Knorr, shot and killed her first husband Clifford Sanders in their tiny one-bedroom house in Galt, near Sacramento. (CONNIE SANDERS)

Howard Sanders' ex-wife Connie with the couple's two sons, Howard Clyde, Jr., 10, and Miles, 7. Connie lived at Theresa's house on Bellingham Way for some time before the deaths of Knorr's daughters. She claims that Theresa has only seen her grandchildren on two occasions. (WENSLEY CLARKSON)

Theresa Knorr kept no photographs of her murdered daughters, so police had to track down out-of-date Sacramento school pictures like this one of Suesan Knorr, aged 14.
(PLACER COUNTY POLICE)

Suesan Knorr's sister, Sheila, aged 15, in a school picture obtained by Placer County investigators shortly after they finally acted upon Terry Knorr's information.
(PLACER COUNTY POLICE)

Theresa Knorr, with ex-Salt Lake City detective Vere Thatcher, whose mother-in-law, Alice Sullivan, was the last elderly woman to be cared for by Theresa before her arrest. This picture was taken at a family party just three days before Placer County investigators arrived at Mrs. Sullivan's home to arrest Knorr for murder. (VERE AND PAT THATCHER)

A Tahoe City Police Department poster released in late 1993 calling for information about the murder of Suesan Knorr, then known only as "Jane Doe" to investigators. This specially re-created photograph was prepared by the National Center for Missing and Exploited Children.

(PLACER COUNTY POLICE)

most of them have blocked Christmas out of their minds completely, and life in Salt Lake City that year could not be greater.

Christmas Eve at Alice Sullivan's neat single-story corner house on 1504 South 600 East was, according to family tradition, when the presents were handed out among twenty-five of the closest family members.

Over the years, Bud Sullivan—with all his years' experience as an executive at the First Interstate Bank, Utah—had devised a sensible system so that no one in the family had to buy gifts for everyone because that would be ludicrously expensive. Instead, the entire family wrote their names on a piece of paper and dropped it into a hat and drew just one name out at a time, so that no one had to purchase more than one present. Naturally, Theresa was included in that.

She sat with the four generations of Sullivans around Alice's vast Christmas tree, flowing with lights and decorations, savoring every moment. Who knows if she even once considered the plight of her surviving children scattered around the country, suffering endless nightmares of the dreadful injuries she allegedly inflicted on them?

On Christmas Day itself, the Sullivans reconvened back at Alice's house for Christmas dinner. Theresa Cross could not believe her luck. The holiday celebrations were continuing, and the family had insisted she stay involved throughout.

Dinner that day consisted of a huge turkey cooked to perfection at Alice's daughter Pat's home just around the corner. Everything else—salads, turkey dressing, apple and pumpkin pies, all the vegetables—were prepared by Theresa Cross in Alice's kitchen. Her own children recalled that mealtimes at home in Sacramento usually consisted of microwave fast food . . . if they were lucky.

The Christmas celebrations that day were rounded off with a bourbon toast for all the adults, including Theresa. Bud Sullivan was impressed that the warm and caring lady looking after his mother only drank alcohol very occasionally. And she had to be forced to accept a drink that day. Bud was surprised that Theresa Cross did not seem to want to say too much about her past, especially her children. But he figured he shouldn't pry, so he never pressed her on the subject.

Bud's sister Pat Thatcher had a little more intuition, and tried to pump Theresa Cross for further information.

But Theresa was very evasive. She did tell Pat she had no daughters, and talked in hushed tones about how she had two sons, but one had been killed in an accident. It was a fantasy, but as with the Cheneys back in Bountiful, how could anyone know she was lying?

Pat had the overriding impression that Theresa Cross was a very private kind of person who made everyone feel they shouldn't ask too many questions.

The only background about Theresa's upbringing came in a brief reference to being brought up on a farm in Iowa. But it was a fleeting comment that she never expanded upon.

Theresa did confide in Pat that she was happy to be working for them and considered them to be her adopted family.

Bud and Pat were eternally grateful to have discov-

ered Theresa. She seemed a real gem. Not many people
would work around the clock without a word of complaint. It was almost as if Theresa was punishing herself
by being so solid and reliable.

Her typical day at Alice Sullivan's house started at
5:00 A.M., when she liked to get up and get things done
about the house before Alice woke up. Often she would
pop out to do some errands in the morning and let Alice sleep in—unlike her previous charge, Alice Powell,
this Alice was fairly active and compos mentis. On returning from her errands, it would be time to get Alice
up, bathe her, and feed her breakfast. However, Theresa spent a lot of time reading in her room in the middle of the day. Both Bud and Pat would often ring the
front door of the house and have to wait some moments before Theresa waddled through the house to
open up. Alice, usually sitting in her favorite chair near
the front window, was not expected to start answering
doorbells.

Pat Thatcher's only concern about Theresa was that
she never seemed to want to take any time off.

Theresa happily took Alice Sullivan to the Our Lady
of Lourdes Catholic Church, on the corner of Eleventh
East and Seventh South most Sundays, and she was
very conscientious about making sure the old lady—
who was eighty-six at the time—got whatever she required.

"Theresa would often call me up and say, 'Your
mother needs this and that.' I would say, 'Fine, Theresa
you go get it and give me the bill and I'll pay you,' "
says Pat.

But her mother's nurse often did not give Pat the bill

—preferring instead to pay for the old lady herself. Frequently, Theresa would spring for a blouse or a pair of shoes for Alice—all paid for with her own hard-earned cash. She made a special effort to make Alice look nice whenever they both ventured out.

On Valentine's Day—February 14, 1993—she even bought Alice a gift to celebrate. Pat, meanwhile, kept saying to herself, "This lady is too good to be true . . ."

Bud Sullivan did find it strange that Theresa Cross spent so much time in her little bedroom at the back of the house, even though she had the run of the place. But he reckoned it was none of his business, so he did not mention it to Theresa.

That nine-by-nine room at the back of the Sullivan house became a virtual shrine to Theresa Cross. It was filled with jewelry and a closet crammed with expensive clothes. That room was the one place she could gather her real thoughts and fears . . . and face the memories of the past. The room itself was always kept immaculately clean. A bedspread colored dark blue, with streaks of blood red, adorned the queen-size bed that was provided by the Sullivans, although Theresa insisted on buying herself a new mattress. Matching drapes were closed for much of the time against the light. Just like back in Sacramento, there were no pictures on the wall, no evidence of family or friends. But on a white cabinet lay a vast range of expensive makeup: Christian Dior, Lancôme, and other designer labels. Under the bed was a box filled with receipts from restaurants, shops, and hotels that she had collected during her travels over the previous few years.

The bills were from as far afield as East Illinois and California. In another box under the bed, yet more makeup. In one corner, a large maple double dresser with a full-length mirror that she would constantly check her appearance in. Inside the dresser, many pairs of shoes, nearly all a safe, one-inch heel. Theresa had so many clothes that Bud had to build her an overspill rail on the enclosed porch outside the back of the house.

Many of her dresses, skirts, and pants were red. Red was her favorite color. It tended to be a very crimson shade of red. The color of blood.

Dozens of books lined the shelf of the white cabinet. They included books on Jews, Catholics, and Mormons. There were also many on the development of new drugs, plus one on herbal medicine. She also had medical manuals that described how to deal with people with Parkinson's and Alzheimer's diseases. Theresa's pride and joy was her own phone line. She had paid almost a hundred dollars to have it installed within days of taking the job at Alice Sullivan's. Sometimes she would spend hours making secretive phone calls in her room.

But, much more surprising, in her double dresser there were at least six wigs. Blond, brunette, red, all lengths and shapes.

The neat, dark-haired bob hairpiece looked just like the hairstyle she had in her Utah driver's license photo.

Neither Pat nor Bud ever recall seeing Theresa Cross wearing any of the wigs. No one has any idea why she kept them.

Theresa Cross's errands were usually carried out before Alice Sullivan woke up, and often included a trip to her local Albertson's Supermarket to stock up on food for the house.

No one knows if she ever noticed the girl at the checkout or if that girl recognized her. For Theresa Knorr's daughter Terry worked at that same Albertson's for most of the first half of 1993.

"They could even have glanced at each other—who knows?" reckoned one of the detectives who interviewed Terry later.

Terry even told investigators: "I felt the presence of my mother nearby. I knew she was close."

Whatever the implications of Terry's "sixth sense" about her mother's close proximity, there were a number of other strange incidents that occurred before Theresa Cross's eventual arrest:

1. Bud Sullivan and his sister Pat Thatcher say that Theresa Cross became much more secretive and reclusive around the beginning of 1993. She also seemed to be spending all her weekly wages, even though she had virtually no living expenses and, according to Bud, must have been capable of saving at least $1000 to $1200 a month.

    Bud's brother-in-law, Vere Thatcher—the ex–Salt Lake City Police detective—speculates that Theresa Cross may have been blackmailed.

2. Why did Howard Sanders suddenly decide to track down his long-lost half brother Billy Bob after more than five years apart? Eventually Howard's new fiancée traced Billy in June 1992, and the two half brothers met up to discuss what to do about their mother.

But William Knorr wanted to just forget the past, according to statements later made to detectives.

3. Howard told the Placer County investigators that he kept in touch with his only surviving half sister, Terry Knorr, through a lawyer called Carl Swain, who is also currently representing Howard's new fiancée in a personal injury suit. How much influence did this have on bringing Theresa Cross to justice, and what messages were passed between the two?

4. According to Howard, Terry called her brother Billy Bob's wife, DeLois, on a number of occasions. These phone calls have been described in police testimony by Howard Sanders as being "threatening." DeLois refused to put her husband Billy Bob on the phone to his sister, and told Terry: "No, you're not getting any money out of Bill. You tell me why you want to get ahold of him?" During the call, Terry just kept repeating: "Let me talk to Bill. Let me talk to Bill."

DeLois later contradicted what Howard had claimed by telling investigators that Terry had called up, but she had pretended to Terry that she had rung up the wrong William Knorr.

5. Why did Robert Knorr Sr. and his son Billy suddenly reunite around this same time, even though they had not been in touch for sixteen years? Billy insisted to investigators shortly after his arrest that on the first night they met, he told his father that Suesan had been found dead in the hills after running away. But why were they talking about it anyway?

At the time of writing, these points remain unanswered. These questions do not suggest that the accounts given to investigators of life inside the Knorr household are inaccurate, but the circumstances behind how they were finally brought to the attention of police may require further inquiries.

By an unfortunate twist of fate, Terry's life in Salt Lake City during 1993 was rapidly becoming as unhappy as her mother's was becoming contented. Living in her husband's family's home was stretching the tolerance levels of all concerned, and police were being called to the house with even more regularity than before.

Terry's only escape had been the job at Albertson's. But if she did catch a glimpse of her mother, then that must have turned into a dreaded place as well.

Then there was Terry's desperation to have children. She was convinced that having a baby might turn her life around. But she also knew that her mother had crushed her stomach so many times that she would have to continue having medical tests before she would know if she could even get pregnant.

Also, Terry was worried that having a child might re-open a much more dangerous scenario. She feared that if she did have children, they might end up being abused in the same awful way that she was. Terry was frightened that her mother might have handed down that propensity for violence to her only surviving daughter. Like mother, like daughter. The very thought haunted her, and it almost resulted in a disaster when a close friend asked Terry if she would look after her two children for a couple of days while her friend went off on a romantic weekend with her husband. Terry agreed because she felt she owed her friend a favor, and she also longed to be in the company of children whom she presumed had actually had a real childhood instead of the brutal regime she had faced day in, day out within the Knorr household.

In fact, Terry was positively excited by the prospect of looking after the youngsters. If anyone had romanticized the very notion of parenthood, it was Terry.

But the first night of looking after those children almost turned into a tragedy. Leaving one of the children alone in the living room while she cooked a meal in the kitchen, Terry did not notice the little boy creep down the stairs to the living quarters of that house in Sandy she shared with her in-laws.

Within minutes she smelled burning. Emerging from the kitchen, she rushed down the spiral staircase and found the little boy in the process of setting fire to her husband's stereo with a box of matches. At first, Terry felt the urge to strike out at the boy.

But then she stopped herself.

She thought she would have been justified in hitting the child, but she also feared what it might lead to. So, instead of harming the child, she immediately made arrangements to get the boy taken elsewhere.

The incident made Terry feel very vulnerable. She had managed to hold herself back from repeating her mother's alleged sins. She knew that traditionally, the abused child tends to end up abusing his or her own children. She wanted to prove she had broken the cycle.

Terry also had to face another aspect of her abuse at the hands of her mother: She still had not brought that woman to justice. God knows, she had tried hard enough.

Watching television one night, she found herself glued to the show, *America's Most Wanted.* Many of the criminals on the lam featured on the program that night had committed crimes even longer ago than Theresa Knorr. She was particularly fascinated by one case in which the tipster bypassed all the usual police officials and went directly to the actual investigators to get some action taken. Terry realized that charges could still be brought against her mother, but she would have to get to the right people.

This time she would do it. She would actually make the first move to get her mother finally brought to justice. No more halfhearted chats with psychiatrists. No more tearful confessions to friends. This time she would directly call the police department that would have dealt with the deaths of her two sisters.

Terry took a map book off the shelf in that dark and dingy house in Sandy and started to look for the town of Truckee, California . . .

Fifteen

"As sick as her love was, she was my
mother and the only person I knew as
loving me."
Terry, only surviving daughter

Police Sergeant Ron Perea, of the Nevada County,
California, Sheriff's Office, was used to taking phone
calls from all sorts of weirdos, but there was something
about the female voice on the other end of the line that
had a ring of authenticity about it.

The caller said that her name was Terry Knorr and
her two sisters had been killed some years earlier and
their bodies dumped in the Nevada County area. Then
Terry mentioned that one of her sisters' remains had
been left in a box. Sergeant Perea immediately remembered the girl the Texan serial killer had confessed to
killing, and his initial impression of the caller altered.
Maybe she was just another makeup artist, an attention
seeker. After all, they had closed that case years earlier.

Then Terry mentioned the fate of her other sister,
and Perea's ears pricked up again because he knew that
his colleagues in neighboring Placer County still had an
open investigation on a charred corpse found about
eight years previously.

At 10:00 A.M. the following morning, October 28,

1993, Sergeant Perea called up Sergeant John Fitzgerald at the Tahoe City substation of the Placer County Sheriff's Office, told him about the call from Terry, and gave him her phone number.

Fitzgerald—forty-six years old, brawny, Brobdingnagian, his mustache freshly trimmed, in his favorite brown tweed sports jacket—was crisply authoritative, a master of cop jargon with a soft, friendly center.

"I'll get right on it."

The detective instantly knew precisely which unsolved case Perea's caller was referring to. He had joined the Tahoe substation as a detective just a year after the discovery of the body. Also, he had only just printed up some brand-new flyers with a specially enhanced photograph of Jane Doe #4873/84, prepared from autopsy photographs by the National Center for Missing and Exploited Children in Arlington, Virginia. The poster, headlined DO YOU KNOW HER? also featured photos of Suesan's ring and one of her earrings.

Fitzgerald picked up the phone almost immediately and tried to contact Terry Knorr. There was no reply. He tried again later in the day—still no answer.

Raised in Panama—his grandfather helped build the canal—John Fitzgerald had an interesting and varied life history. His family settled in the U.S. from Ireland four generations back. He went to a small private school. Then, just as he was about to go to college, the Vietnam War came along. "I was a plane captain in the Navy on the USS *Independence* aircraft carrier," he explained. "That's the guy who's in charge of a particular plane, inspecting it before and after service." He spent four years in Vietnam, and placed that experience in an interesting perspective by commenting that "basically, I saw no action. I was out at sea the whole time." After his discharge in 1970, he enrolled in college and became a reserve police officer. He studied criminal justice, graduated from Sierra College, near Auburn, California, and went to work for the Rosewood Police Department, just east of Sacramento. Fitzgerald was anxious to make his mark, but he wanted to do it cleanly, without owing favors and without compromising his ethics. He was a true son of the 1960s.

Fitzgerald moved over to work for the Plumas County Police Department before switching to the Roosevelt Police Department, and then took the job of detective up at the Placer County Sheriff's Department nine years ago. Married for the second time, with five children between him and his wife, Fitzgerald is a cop with a heart that he openly wears on the sleeve of his always immaculately pressed shirt.

At 4:45 P.M. that day, a female came on the phone who identified herself as Terry Knorr. Close to tears, she repeated her account of life under her tyrannical mother and the eventual tragedy of her sisters' killings.

As Fitzgerald later recalled: "She started talking and talking. I'd call it nonstop verbal diarrhea."

Fitzgerald sat on the other end of the line, transfixed by the gruesome account of life in Sacramento. Terry disclosed incidents like being locked in a freezer, having knives thrown at them, being handcuffed to the table and beaten, being hung from the door, suffering regular kickings from her mother, being burned by cigarettes.

Then she spoke about the force-feeding, the hot bowl burning the inside of her sister's legs, the molestation by her father, the time her mother stood on her sister's neck.

Terry even gave Fitzgerald the locations where all this occurred: 5539 Bellingham Way, Orangevale, and then the tiny house off 2410 Auburn Boulevard.

"She was very excitable. She was fed up of people not listening to her. She desperately wanted to get the whole thing off her chest," said Fitzgerald.

Then, weeping periodically, Terry went into graphic detail about the deaths of her two sisters, even describing how the family was spooked when that bird hit the windshield on the way back from burning Suesan's body.

The conversation went on for an hour and a half. Toward the end of the call, Fitzgerald started to test the authenticity of her claims by asking Terry questions that only someone close to the case of the burned body at Squaw Valley could possibly know.

"Describe to me the ring that your sister was wearing," asked Fitzgerald.

"It had three rows of diamonds," came the accurate reply.

"What about other jewelry?"

"She had earrings with bells on them."

And so it went. Every time Fitzgerald asked a tricky question, Terry came back with the perfect answer.

Fitzgerald was fairly certain about Terry. But there was one final question about his Jane Doe that had always baffled him and all the detectives who had handled the case over the years.

"Why did she have those diapers in her possession?" asked the detective.

Terry's reply set her off on yet another graphic description, this time of Suesan's miserable last few weeks of existence.

For John Fitzgerald, this was a major breakthrough on a case he had personally continued to pursue even though it had remained unsolved for more than nine years. He knew that Terry's sister Suesan had to be that Jane Doe Case #4873/84.

In an extraordinary coincidence, he had only just been in touch with the producers of TV's *America's Most Wanted* to ask them to run a segment about that Jane Doe in a last desperate effort to try and identify her.

Suddenly, out of nowhere, a homicide investigation was about to take a dramatic turn.

"This time something will be done," Fitzgerald assured Terry. "I want to come and talk to you in person. I'll call you tomorrow."

At 10:00 A.M. the next morning, John Fitzgerald drove his gray Ford Explorer along the winding lane that leads past a dozen trailers to the tiny house attached to the apartment block just off Auburn Boulevard, where Terry said she had witnessed death and destruction at the hands of her mother and brothers.

When he got no reply from the house, he tracked down Fern Drake, the manager of the complex, and asked her if she recalled whether a family called the Knorrs had ever lived at the house.

"That name sounds familiar. It must have been them

that rented the place. I evicted them eight years back," explained Fern, who assured Fitzgerald she would try and locate her rental records to confirm the exact dates the family lived at the house.

Next, Fitzgerald headed for the house on Bellingham Way, Orangevale. That also checked out.

By 3:00 P.M. that afternoon, John Fitzgerald was completely and utterly convinced that Terry's claims were accurate. He contacted Inspector Johnnie Smith, his boss at the Placer County Sheriff's headquarters in Auburn, and advised him of all the details.

Smith—a twenty-six-year vet with a droll sense of humor and a sharp eye for detail—felt a chill run up the back of his neck the moment he heard the name Theresa Knorr.

"Hell. I worked a case involving her back in 'eighty-three," he told an astonished Fitzgerald.

Smith then recounted that interview with Theresa Knorr about her sister's murder and the subsequent surveillance operation on the house just off Auburn. The moment he had made the connection, he told Fitzgerald that they should both get up to Salt Lake City as quickly as possible.

Terry Groves (her married name) was surprised, but also relieved to hear from Fitzgerald that afternoon that he and Smith were flying up the very next day. She was actually starting to believe that her mother might really be brought to justice.

At 7:00 A.M. the next morning, October 30, John Fitzgerald met Johnnie Smith at the Placer County Sheriff's Department in Auburn and set off to Sacramento Airport in Fitzgerald's Ford Explorer. It was the day before Halloween and Fitzgerald had become embroiled in an alleged double murder that, if true, would turn out to be as gruesome and satanistic as those devil worshipers in Salem, Massachusetts, who sparked the tradition of Halloween three hundred years ago.

By 1:15 P.M. the two detectives were knocking on the tatty white front door of the house in Sandy, near Salt Lake City, where Terry lived with husband Mike and her in-laws. She greeted them and took them downstairs to the basement annex where she lived, and made them a cup of coffee.

Both detectives were intrigued to finally be meeting Terry. She was more upbeat than they had expected. Somehow, through all that pain and anguish, she still had lively, sparkling blue eyes and a round, healthy face.

For at least fifteen minutes all three made polite small talk, managing to awkwardly avoid mentioning the very subject the two cops had flown from California to discuss. The niceties were harshly broken when one of the cops asked Terry if she had any children.

"Nope. Probably can't have 'em because of the beatings she gave me."

Smith and Fitzgerald looked stunned for a moment. That was the signal. Fitzgerald placed his Dictaphone on the table in front of them and they began the interview.

Terry took them through her entire childhood. Most of it was pretty grim stuff. It seemed as though beatings were carried out on a daily basis.

After Terry had described the killings, Fitzgerald

started questioning her about certain evidence taken from the area near Suesan's body. As he showed her photographs of her dead sister's jewelry, she spotted Suesan's ring. It sparked a vision in Terry's mind. She shouted at Fitzgerald and Smith:

"This is my sister's ring. I want that ring."

"This is a black and white picture of a ring," said Fitzgerald calmly and carefully, so that it would be clearly stated on the tape recorder.

"I want that ring," repeated Terry emotionally.

A few moments later, through all the gruesome details of her life, Terry even identified the Budweiser beer can found close to her sister's charred remains.

Terry was fascinated by that flyer Fitzgerald had printed up only a few weeks before her call. She told the investigators that the specially enhanced photograph looked more like her than her sister Suesan.

Three and a half hours after turning on the Dictaphone, the two detectives decided to wind up the interview. They were certain they had both just embarked on the most appalling double homicide investigation either of them had ever encountered.

"I'm going to be working this case and nothing else till we solve it. I promise you," Fitzgerald told Terry as he and Smith left the house that day. He knew she needed constant reassurance.

The details described by Terry had been so riveting and outrageous that neither detective had kept a close eye on the time, and they had less than an hour to get to Salt Lake City Airport, check in, and board the 6:00 P.M. flight back to Sacramento.

The journey to the airport in their rented white compact was a hairy ride through thick rush-hour traffic. They got there with only minutes to spare.

At 10:00 A.M. the next day, safely back in his office at the Tahoe City substation, Fitzgerald called Terry in Sandy to run over a few more points that had arisen after he began analyzing his lengthy interview with her the previous day. Essentially, he needed background details like the places where both sisters had been born. Once again he assured Terry that this time something would be done. "We will find your mother, I promise you," said Fitzgerald.

He then contacted District Attorney Dan Dong to tell him the details of the case. Fitzgerald followed this by starting extensive background checks on Theresa Knorr and her two sons. Terry had given him dates of births, but they had no locations for either Theresa Knorr or Robert, and only a vague area for William. Within hours they located William's workplace and put a surveillance unit on him for a few days to see how he led his life.

Fitzgerald also got in touch with Kelly Keon, the current occupant of that little house just off Auburn Boulevard where so much terror was allegedly inflicted by Theresa Knorr. She immediately agreed to Fitzgerald's request to come and inspect the premises the following day.

At 1:30 P.M. the next day, November 1, Smith and Fitzgerald met with their boss, Sheriff Don Nunes. Their biggest problem was which force should be responsible for the investigation. Sheila's body had actually been found in Nevada County. But, argued Smith and Fitzgerald, her murder had allegedly been committed in that house, and the family had traveled through Placer County on their way to the dump site. Eventually, after some more discussion, it was agreed that Placer County should run the entire operation.

They decided to immediately set up a task force consisting of Smith, Fitzgerald, and Lieutenant Chal DeCecco.

Case status: Open. Investigation to continue, wrote Fitzgerald in his Placer County Sheriff's Department report at the end of that day.

At 8:00 A.M. next morning, Fitzgerald, Smith, and DeCecco—the Knorr investigation task force—met at the Placer County Sheriff's Department in Auburn to discuss how to handle the case inquiries. It was decided that Fitzgerald and DeCecco would:

- Examine the floor of the closet where Sheila had been kept prisoner.
- Try to obtain photographs of both girls from the schools they attended.
- Visit the movie theater where Billy Bob had been employed during the time of the alleged murders.
- Contact the Department of Justice and the Sacramento Post Office to try and get a current location for Theresa Knorr.

Numerous other tasks were discussed at that meeting, but the detectives agreed that these four inquiries were top priority.

The rest of that morning was spent running computer checks on Theresa and Robert Knorr in an attempt to hunt them down. Fitzgerald and DeCecco also visited

La Entrada School and the Mira Loma School, where they obtained photographs of Suesan Knorr and Sheila Sanders.

At 4:00 P.M. Fitzgerald and DeCecco went to the house off Auburn Boulevard and found, to their disappointment, that the interior of the property had been completely redesigned since the fire lit by Terry more than seven years earlier. However, Fitzgerald did find the closet in the hallway where he believed poor Sheila must have been kept prisoner. It had been neatly carpeted over.

Fitzgerald explained to the new tenant, Kelly Keon, that he would like to remove the floor from the closet because it might be possible evidence. She readily agreed, and an arrangement was made for officers to return the next day. Kelly Keon was very cooperative with the detectives and even told them she would leave the key to the front door by her faucet out front so they could let themselves in the next day because she would be out.

That same afternoon, the two investigators contacted Donna Treibel, the manager of the movie theater on Ethan Way where Billy Bob had worked. She could not get access to records to confirm his previous employment, but Fitzgerald was more interested in the shapes and colors of the popcorn-cup boxes delivered to the theater. He accompanied Donna to the storeroom of the theater, only to find that the boxes were nothing like the one used to transport Sheila's body in.

However, Donna then suggested that she might have the kind of box Fitzgerald was looking for at her own house. She promised to get back to him the following day. The investigation was on track again.

The next day, November 3, Fitzgerald made his first breakthrough in trying to track down Theresa Knorr. A computer check came up with her name under a Utah driver's license with an address of 2090 Michigan Avenue, Salt Lake City.

Fitzgerald was astounded. Mother and daughter appeared to be living just a few miles from each other.

He immediately contacted the Salt Lake City Police Department, spoke with Detective Jill Candland, and asked her if a check could be made on that address at Michigan Avenue. She called back a short time later, having been unable to come up with anything that would link Theresa Knorr to that property. Detective Candland promised to make further checks and assured Fitzgerald she would get back to him within a couple of days.

It was frustrating for the Knorr task force. For every three steps forward, they seemed to take two steps back. But that is the nature of these sorts of inquiries. It's painstaking and it's slow, but you hope to get there in the end.

On the same afternoon, Donna Treibel, manager of the movie theater, called Fitzgerald to confirm Billy Bob's employment at the cinema. But the box she found at home seemed to be too small to be the kind that the detective was looking for. Once again Fitzgerald felt a twinge of disappointment.

Then, purely as an afterthought, Donna mentioned that a girlfriend of William Knorr's still worked at the theater. Fitzgerald's enthusiasm jumped right back into gear.

The pieces in the jigsaw were beginning to fit together. The investigation was gradually gaining momentum. Fitzgerald just had to keep it going in the right direction.

On the morning of November 4, 1993, the investigators filed felony complaint number A27527 in the Placer County Municipal Court, alleging two violations of the section 187(a) of the California Penal Code, MURDER and two violations of sections 182(a) (1)/187(a) of the California Penal Code, CONSPIRACY TO COMMIT MURDER for victims Suesan Marline Knorr and Sheila Gay Sanders. The complaint further alleged the special circumstances of MULTIPLE MURDERS and MURDER WAS ESPECIALLY HEINOUS pursuant to California Penal Code sections 190.2 (a) (3) and 190.2(a) (14).

(On November 16 that original complaint was refiled with the special circumstance of MURDER WAS ESPECIALLY HEINOUS deleted and replaced by TORTURE—MURDER.)

That afternoon, as planned, Fitzgerald, DeCecco, and a maintenance crew including special evidence technicians, let themselves into the house just off Auburn Boulevard.

As evidence technicians Kelly Yarborough and Tammy Harris snapped furiously away with their cameras, the crew began to remove the floor of the closet very slowly and gently so as not to risk ruining any vital evidence.

Meanwhile, in the basement, DeCecco and Fitzgerald used hand spotlights to methodically check for any further clues. Inside both their minds was the fear that maybe there would be other bodies. Thankfully, that was not the case.

A few minutes later, John Fitzgerald found himself watching the entire closet-floor removal operation in an almost trancelike state. He could not stop thinking about Terry's vivid description of her sister's withered and crushed body crumpled up in that fetal position. Those haunting visions also reminded him that Terry had mentioned how the closet had a door handle that could only be locked from the outside. He looked at the closet the technicians were so painstakingly removing— it had no such handle.

Fitzgerald then noticed another much smaller closet at the other side of the hallway. It could not have been more than two feet by two and a half feet. He looked inside and saw that it had several shelves. Then he examined the door and realized it had a lock that could easily be the same one as Terry had described.

Fitzgerald went back to examine the other, larger closet. He was starting to doubt his mind. There was only one way to be absolutely sure. He picked up the phone and called Terry in Salt Lake City.

"It's the smaller one just outside the bathroom on the right side," was all Terry had to tell Fitzgerald to assure him that his instincts were correct.

The evidence technicians were stunned when Fitzgerald told them to start all over on the smaller closet. None of them could believe that any human being existed in such a small space.

Sixteen

> Homicide is a function of both person
> and circumstance. We are all capable of
> killing under some circumstances, and
> none of us kills under all circumstances.
> Charles Patrick Ewing, Author

On the west side of Sacramento, at the Target Ware-house Distribution Center in Woodland, two Placer County investigators were speaking to a very curious William Knorr about the death of his aunt, Rosemary Norris, in 1983. The entire interview was conducted purely to sound out Knorr, to see how he would react to an approach by a police officer.

"He was fine. Acted completely normally. He did not have any idea why we were really there," said one of the investigators later.

But then why should William Knorr be suspicious? He had turned over a new leaf, married a pretty girl, settled down in a comfortable home, and avoided all criminal temptations. He had gone his way and Robert had gone in completely the opposite direction. William had a safe, secure life now . . . for the moment.

At 5:00 P.M. that same day, Fitzgerald went and saw William's one-time live-in lover Emily Lewis at the movie theater where she still worked. She told Fitzgerald she no longer knew Billy Bob but was able to recall conversations she had with him about his sister's disappearance. She also gave the detective some important information about where Knorr had worked at other jobs.

At precisely the same time, investigators Smith and Fulenwider were knocking on the door of apartment 38, 9127 Newhall Drive, Sacramento—the home of Theresa Knorr's oldest son, Howard Sanders.

Thirty years old and about to embark on his second marriage, Howard Sanders was disarmingly frank in his statement to Smith and Fulenwider. The two policemen started the interview on a traditional softly, softly approach, building gradually up to the most important points.

About fifteen minutes into the interview, Johnnie Smith decided to press Howard harder about the realities of life inside the Knorr household. It was subtle but very effective:

SMITH: I got the feeling that you wanted to tell us something. You said there had been some weird things happening in your family.
SANDERS: Yeah, well . . .
SMITH: What is weird that's happened that you wanted to talk about?
SANDERS: Well, you know, there's been a lot of, you know, a lot of problems in our family, you know, we all should be pretty much a loony tune . . .

The two detectives hoped that marked the point when they broke through Howard Sanders's reticence.

But not even they could have realized just how much he was going to tell them.

When Sanders faltered again about thirty minutes later, after it came to discussing the witchcraft inside the house, Inspector Smith, dour yet determined, would not let him off the hook.

The investigator started referring to how he had taken lessons in body language. "I still think there's something that you want to tell me that you're holding back . . ."

It worked. Sanders admitted he was holding things back. That second piece of gentle intimidation eventually opened up such a vast torrent of revelations that the two detectives could barely keep up as Sanders mentioned beatings, burnings, whippings, and his own disturbing admission about committing incest with Terry.

But there was one more aspect that neither Smith nor Fulenwider had even the remotest clue about. In another interview with Sanders thirteen days later, he admitted sexually abusing his brother Robert as well as Terry.

Even these two hardened detectives were stunned by his confession. Charges of sexual abuse had been there all the time, like a fire deep in the hold of a ship, sending wisps of smoke and acrid smells curling to the deck. But now this throbbing menace was about to explode without warning and roar up hidden passageways to sink the entire vessel.

By admitting those awful sexual attacks on his brother and sister, Howard Sanders was trying at last to deal with it and then hopefully put out the flames forever.

The following day, Fitzgerald met at the Sheriff's Department with his colleagues Johnnie Smith, Chal DeCecco, and Detective Karl Fulenwider. After discussing their follow-up tasks, they made arrangements to meet with the district attorney in order to obtain a search warrant for William Knorr's home. They also needed to arrange for the issuing of arrest warrants for all three suspects: Theresa Jimmie Knorr, William Robert Knorr, and Robert Wallace Knorr.

Later that morning, John Fitzgerald gave a verbal affidavit to Judge Garbolino at the courthouse in Auburn and officially obtained the search warrant plus the arrest warrants. It was decided that an arrest should be made of William Knorr as quickly as possible, in case he was tipped off about the murder inquiries.

Investigators had gotten to the point where they did not know where the other brother and the mother were, so they needed to arrest William promptly.

At 2:00 P.M. that afternoon, all four detectives traveled to the Target Warehouse Distribution Center in Woodland to arrest William Knorr. Smith drove in his small blue four-door Mercury with Fulenwider, while Fitzgerald and DeCecco traveled in the Explorer. On arrival at the plant, all four detectives initially feared their suspect was not at work because there was no sign of his car in the company parking lot.

But when Smith and his partner went into the personnel office, they were told that Knorr was at work. He had been given a ride in by a friend. The manager was then asked to page Knorr without informing him what it was about. The other two investigators sealed off the rear exit to the building in case Knorr tried to flee.

Five minutes later a bemused-looking William Knorr arrived in the front office, where Johnnie Smith approached him.

"We have a warrant for your arrest," Smith told Knorr.

It took a few moments to sink in. Then William Knorr surprised the officers by asking them if he could call the guy he car-pooled with to tell him not to bother coming by to pick him up on the way home that evening. That was his main concern, rather than the fact he was under arrest for murder.

Three minutes after that, a grim-faced William Knorr was led from the building, where he was turned over by Smith to Fitzgerald and DeCecco, who read Knorr 821/ 822 of the Penal Code regarding magistrate's advisement. Knorr immediately agreed to accompany the officers to the Placer County Sheriff's Department. They snapped a pair of handcuffs on his wrists.

The two detectives began to interview Knorr virtually the moment the three got in Fitzgerald's gun-metal-gray Explorer, and read him his Miranda rights. He was astonished to discover that the interview about his aunt's death the previous day had just been an excuse to get close to him.

During the thirty-minute ride from Woodland to Auburn, Knorr told the detectives that both his sisters had disappeared and he had no idea where his mother or brother were now living. He talked openly about how his mother had abused all the children, and even confirmed that she did own the Ford LTD Terry had mentioned in her statement.

But Knorr was in complete denial as far as the deaths of his two sisters were concerned. He would not concede anything about them.

Then, just as Fitzgerald drove the Explorer through Auburn toward the Sheriff's Department on the other side of town, William Knorr mentioned that he had been threatened with death by his mother if he ever tried to leave the family unit.

The two investigators sat in silence, hoping he would elaborate. But William Knorr did not say anything more. Moments later they parked outside the Sheriff's Department.

On arrival inside the building, DeCecco escorted William Knorr to the investigation interview room. Knorr was being fairly cooperative, but still not candid about the actual allegations against him. A tape recorder and a video camera were permanently set up in the room to monitor all interviews.

William Knorr flatly denied any involvement in the disappearance of Sheila or Suesan. Then Fitzgerald and DeCecco advised him that they had already interviewed his sister Terry and half brother Howard.

"We kinda put our cards on the table," said John Fitzgerald, ever the master of the understatement. "We wanted him to know that we knew what had happened."

William Knorr looked worried. He immediately recalled for the two investigators a number of incidents inside the Knorr household, even claiming Suesan was out of control and turning tricks as a prostitute and that was why Theresa Knorr started beating her. He talked about how Suesan was trapped under the table on that kitchen floor.

William Knorr insisted to the detectives that when they took Suesan off into the mountains, his mother had simply informed them that they were "going on a car ride." He also said—contrary to what Terry claimed —that Terry was in the car with them. He confirmed that the first trip had been aborted, and told them about loading Suesan into his mother's Ford LTD the next day and once again setting off east on Interstate 80.

John Fitzgerald later confronted Terry about her brother's claims that she had been in the car when both her sisters were dumped. She denied it categorically.

William Knorr even admitted to the two officers that he doused his sister in gasoline and then lit the fatal match. For the second time, he insisted his mother had threatened him with death if he should decide to tell anyone about that night's activities.

"What about Sheila?" the investigators asked their suspect. William claimed he was once again ordered to help dispose of her by his evil mother. William said Sheila was not alive when they removed her body from the closet.

Then he revealed that just before the family dumped Sheila, they stopped by the side of the road to look for potential locations to leave the box containing her body and were spotted by a passing police cruiser.

As the two brothers scanned the bleak and darkened terrain a few yards from the Ford LTD, two patrolman approached Theresa Knorr, who was still sitting behind the wheel. They asked her what she was doing out in a deserted area late at night.

"The two boys are just over there urinating," came Theresa Knorr's very calm reply.

The two policemen accepted her response and did not even stop to inspect the contents of the trunk of that car. If they had opened it up, they would have found the box containing Sheila's withered corpse and prevented her alleged killers from keeping their liberty for more than eight years.

As the interview at the sheriff's headquarters drew to a close, William Knorr insisted to the investigators that he had cut himself off from the family and did not want to remember any more facts about the deaths of his two sisters. But he did admit that he had not intended to ever tell authorities about the two deaths.

Meanwhile, Smith and Fulenwider traveled to William Knorr's home at 4016 Tressler Avenue, North Highlands, where they told his wife, DeLois Ann Knorr, that her husband had just been arrested for murder. She was stunned by the news, but agreed to help detectives with some background information.

DeLois—a pretty, slimly built blonde with a preference for neat, tight-fitting power suits and two-inch heels—told the investigators she had never met William's mother and that her husband had told her that she had been very abusive toward the children.

She also revealed to detectives that William Knorr told her that one of his sisters had been climbing on a shelf after being ordered to do so by his mother and that his sister fell and broke her neck.

By 3:35 P.M. Fulenwider and Smith were executing their search warrant at William Knorr's home after reassuring a very shocked DeLois that it had to be done.

An hour later the two investigators encountered Robert Knorr Sr., who had been alerted to the situation by DeLois. His first response to the detectives was not horror at the news of the arrests, but a mild concern that two of the Veterans' Administration payment checks sent to Theresa Knorr to help Terry once she turned eighteen had been returned.

Knorr Sr. informed detectives that, apart from William, he had not seen his kids in seventeen years.

Then the father of Suesan Knorr told investigators that Theresa Knorr never liked Sheila. He insisted that his ex-wife had hit and beaten Sheila on a regular basis, and he recalled one particular incident when Sheila was about three years old and Theresa Knorr beat the little girl's head so hard against a wall he had had to intervene.

Neither of the investigators responded openly to Knorr's remarks, but privately they were starting to wonder why no one had ever brought Theresa Knorr to justice years before she began allegedly killing her daughters.

Back at the Placer County Sheriff's Department, methodical computer checks had finally uncovered a possible location for Robert Knorr—the Nevada State Jail, at Ely. No one was that surprised to find Robert was already incarcerated for the murder of a bartender, completely unconnected with the abuse and killings alleged to have taken place inside the Knorr household. Or was it?

The Knorr task force decided not to rush across the state line to interview Robert. He had nowhere to run. Their main priority was to locate Theresa Knorr before she completely disappeared under a haze of false names and disguises.

At 2:30 P.M. the following day, November 5, Fitzgerald and DeCecco went to see William Knorr, this time in his cell at the Placer County Jail attached to the main courtrooms in Auburn. Again William was read his Miranda rights before DeCecco switched on a Dictaphone minicassette recorder.

The two detectives wanted to go over some of the other details surrounding Knorr's sisters' deaths, like the type of duct tape used to wrap around Suesan's body and across her mouth. Knorr insisted that he could not remember any shooting incident involving Suesan or any other wounds inflicted by his mother or Suesan.

He did talk about the dreadful, last beating inflicted on Sheila by her mother, and he referred to the locations where the bodies were dumped after being shown a number of crime scene photos by Fitzgerald.

That same day, the Placer County Sheriff's Department issued a two-page press release to inform the world of the extraordinary double murder inquiry. Written in heavy, bold-type capital letters, it began:

SHERIFF DONALD J. NUNES RELEASES THE FOLLOWING INFORMATION:

SHERIFF NUNES ANNOUNCED TODAY THAT A 1984 HOMICIDE, ONE OF THE MOST ALARMING AND BIZARRE IN THE HISTORY OF PLACER COUNTY, HAS BEEN RESOLVED . . .

The release went on to notify the media of all the case's basic details and then signed off with a piece of guessology that was pretty close to the mark:

THERESA KNORR MAY BE EMPLOYED, OR SEEKING EM-
PLOYMENT, AT A CONVALESCENT HOSPITAL.

That same day, Fitzgerald—still very concerned that he had no concrete clues as to where Theresa Knorr was living—contacted police in Washoe County, Nevada, to see if they could locate her in the Reno area. He had been told by prison officials in Ely that Robert Knorr had tried to contact his mother at an address in Reno. Detective Dick Williamson, of the Washoe County Sheriff's Department, assured Fitzgerald he would do everything possible to help try and track down Theresa Knorr, and promised to get back to him as quickly as possible.

Fitzgerald also contacted Terry once again to discuss the progress he was making. He asked her to make a list of all the incidents of abuse suffered by her and her sisters at the hands of their mother and two brothers, William and Robert.

Then Fitzgerald told Terry he would be in touch with her "in a few weeks." The investigator's words summed up Terry's worst fears. When he said "a few weeks," she began to wonder if the police were really that interested. The lack of urgency in Fitzgerald's response worried her. She had come this far. She wanted action to be taken immediately. But they still had not even located her mother. She was very, very worried.

Seventeen

"You know all she did was screw her
own life. For Christ's sake, do you
think, I mean, if I had, I mean I'm
going right now through surgeries to try
to have children because of the abuse.
My insides were mangled from this
woman. Yet, my mother also did some
wonderful things."

Terry Knorr

"I'll get you. I know where you are."

The male voice on the other end of the telephone
was calm, dry, and very menacing. Terry was extremely
nervous. She slammed the handset down without uttering a word. It had only been a few hours since Sergeant
Fitzgerald had informed her he would be in touch with
her in a few weeks.

In a few weeks I could be dead, thought Terry.

A couple of minutes later—at just about 9:00 P.M. on
November 5, 1993—the telephone rang again. This time
Terry hesitated to pick it up. But it kept on ringing re-
lentlessly. She succumbed.

"I'll get you. I know where you are."

She slammed it down again. This time Terry was petrified. She picked up the phone and called the local

police department at Sandy and got through to desk duty officer Jeff Duval.

Within a few hours he had placed a flag on the house, just in case any strangers were lurking nearby.

The following morning, thirty-four-year-old Sandy Police Department detective David Lundberg was enjoying a lazy Saturday at home when his sergeant, Eddie Kantor, called to ask him if he would be prepared to talk to a lady about some threatening phone calls that she claimed were linked to the murder of her two sisters.

"We need to look into this to see if there is anything in it," Kantor told Lundberg.

The young detective was intrigued. He called Terry at the number she had left with Officer Duval the previous evening. Lundberg listened patiently for more than an hour as she poured out her life story once again.

After getting off the phone with Terry, Lundberg immediately contacted John Fitzgerald in Placer County, who confirmed the existence of the task force. Both cops assumed that Terry's plea to her local police was an attempt to guarantee that this time something really was going to be done.

Lundberg went into the Sandy Police Department that Saturday morning and did some computer checks on Terry's home address. He soon discovered that police had been called to the house on at least a dozen occasions, and only two weeks earlier, Terry had even spent a night in jail after an altercation with a patrolman who tried to break up a domestic disturbance at the house.

*   *   *

David Lundberg's devotion was typical of a man with a very clear sense of right and wrong. The last of nine kids brought up in Salt Lake City, the dapper detective wanted to be a cop "because I got into a lot of trouble as a kid and decided it might be kinda fun to join the other side." His problems included involvement in drugs, hanging out and drinking beer. Then he did two years at college studying law enforcement, and joined the Sandy Police Department. Married life beckoned once . . . for just three months. "Thank God it was a quick one." Now he shares his neat house on the edge of Sandy with a couple of cats and a dog.

Lundberg's biggest case was the Alta View Hospital siege in Sandy in 1990. "They made a TV movie out of that one," he says proudly. Then a young patrolman, Lundberg arrived on the scene not realizing that a siege was in progress, and immediately found himself confronting an armed man who was holding two nurses hostage. The gunman, furious at Lundberg for daring to challenge him, then killed one of the nurses to prove he meant business. "It was very traumatic." After eight hours, the siege ended and gunman Richard Worthington was arrested. "He hung himself in jail recently," said Lundberg, with just a touch of satisfaction in his voice.

When Lundberg arrived at Terry's place in his tan-colored Corsica the following Monday morning, he immediately recognized the property as the same place he had visited as a patrolman during yet another of Terry's regular domestic disturbances a year or so earlier.

Terry was relieved to have another policeman take an

interest in her case. The combination of the threatening phone calls and John Fitzgerald's comment about getting back to her in a few weeks had made her feel as if no one really cared.

The young, ambitious detective was even more intrigued when Terry told him she had reported the killings to a sheriff over at Woods Cross three years earlier and that nothing was done. Terry also revealed that she had told one of his colleagues at the Sandy Police Department, who had called at the house following yet another domestic disturbance at least a year earlier.

Lundberg bonded very well with the frightened twenty-three-year-old. He was especially interested in her claims because he had worked a number of child abuse cases over the years.

"The more detail she went into, the more convinced I became," said Lundberg. "I was fascinated."

In the background, Terry's in-laws drifted in and out of the room, hardly uttering a word. Lundberg says he felt they were very suspicious of his motives in coming to the house. The detective's only aim was in fact to ensure that this time Terry's claims were properly acted upon. He was also determined to expose the officers from Woods Cross and Sandy who had apparently ignored Terry's plight.

Terry was very impressed by David Lundberg. By the end of their meeting, she felt that the young detective really did care about what she was saying.

Lundberg even gave Terry his home phone number and insisted that she feel free to call him anytime.

"I had a gut feeling about Terry. If I was dealing with

a dangerous suspect, then it would be different, but this was a case where she really needed someone to talk to."

As Lundberg left Terry's house, he promised her he would get something done. As they stood on the doorstep, he stopped momentarily and hugged Terry reassuringly.

"If you need anything, call me."

The moment Lundberg got back to his neat, pristine desk at the ultramodern, open-plan detectives' bureau at the Sandy Police Department's brand-new headquarters on Centennial Parkway, alongside Interstate 15, he put a request in to find out who interviewed Terry all those years earlier.

The department CAD computer system was supposed to log all police-involved incidents. It records addresses, times, dates, and people's names, to provide data to be cross-referenced with police departments across the nation.

Lundberg punched in a request for everything on Terry's home address at Pepperwood Drive. Within minutes he was poring over the many details of the domestic disputes at the house, but there was no mention of an interview into the deaths of her sisters. Lundberg wondered if Terry had perhaps mentioned it to an officer who wrote it off during one of those many visits by saying she was intoxicated and talking nonsense.

A few days later, after conducting his own unofficial internal inquiries, Lundberg tracked down the Sandy policeman concerned and confronted him.

"He looked me in the face and said he did not recall her saying anything about her sisters," says Lundberg bitterly. He believes that cop was "covering his ass like a true professional."

The next day, Lundberg returned to Terry's home to try and get some more details about her allegations. She was more relaxed because the threatening phone calls had stopped. Terry even admitted her own innermost fears about becoming a child abuser herself. It really worried Terry that she might end up like her mom, and she told him how she had gotten that friend to take the child away who almost burned down the house when she was babysitting.

Lundberg gave Terry a poster that says LOVE DOESN'T HAVE TO HURT, which featured a photo of a hand holding a rose with just a prick of blood on the forefinger. Below it read: *Domestic Violence* Can *Stop 1–800–897–LINK.* He knew that if a similar sort of service had existed a few years earlier, the Knorr tragedy might have been prevented.

Having observed the poverty inside that house on Pepperwood, Lundberg also insisted Terry and her in-laws have his Thanksgiving turkey voucher, awarded to all serving police officers at Sandy as a gesture of thanks from City Hall.

Lundberg believes that Terry was feeling isolated because John Fitzgerald and the Placer County task force were a long distance away.

Terry frequently would call him in the middle of the night with a nugget of information she had forgotten to tell him before.

"She was always very apologetic, saying, 'I hope I did not disturb you or wake you up.' "

Lundberg spent hours one morning making calls to

all the hospitals in the Salt Lake City area to find Terry a friendly, sympathetic psychiatrist willing to treat her for no charge. He recognized that she was someone in dire need of professional counseling.

The Nevada State Prison, at Ely, is the sort of place where inmates sometimes bolt across the day-room floor and, at full stride, smash their fists into the side of a prison guard's head, knocking him to the floor.

But the obvious problems of life inside a tough jail had shrunk into insignificance for twenty-four-year-old Robert Wallace Knorr. As he paced up and down the nine-by-nine cell he shared with another inmate, he could not stop thinking about what was happening back in Auburn.

The police had already been in touch with him and asked for his full cooperation. He turned them down flat, and one investigator predicted that authorities were going to have to get a court order to force him to appear in any eventual trial. They already knew that the whole question of whether or not he should be treated as an adult or a child was going to be a crucial part of any court hearing, as he was fifteen and sixteen at the times of his sisters' killings.

A few days after Terry received those threatening phone calls, her mother, Theresa Knorr, noticed the first newspaper and television reports concerning Terry's allegations against her. Sheriff Don Nunes's press release on the investigation into Sheila and Suesan's deaths had alerted the world to her alleged crimes.

But it was the local news report on Utah's KUTV Channel 2 that must have shaken even Theresa Knorr to the very core. There, on the television screen, was her only surviving daughter, Terry, telling the world about the awful abuse and murder allegedly inflicted on her family.

Terry, close to tears throughout the interview, told interviewer Peter Rosen: "What kind of mother would do that? What kind of person am I going to be for the rest of my life because of this?

"All my life I've tried to put out of my mind what happened. I couldn't believe that it actually happened. I just want my sisters to know I had nothing to do with this and I loved them. I don't have them now and I want them back.

"I told all these people, but none of them wanted to believe I was actually telling the truth. They all thought I had loony tunes and that I had problems, well, what the heck do they expect!

"I have asked myself a hundred times why didn't I just tell them to run. I didn't know what to do. All my life I have tried to block it out of my mind."

The KUTV Channel 2 news show also reported that police were still trying to find Theresa Jimmie Knorr. Fitzgerald had even provided the media with a copy of that almost glamorous photograph of her that she used on her Utah driver's license. Sheriff Nunes admitted: "We don't know where she is. She's in the wind somewhere."

On the morning of November 5, Theresa Knorr got a loan in the form of a check from Bud Sullivan for $4600 to be paid back to him against her salary. He had turned down her initial request a week earlier. But then she came back to him and said she really needed the money. Bud—a relaxed good old boy in his early sixties —asked her why. She told him she had another heavy tax bill to pay, and since she had reliably repaid an earlier loan out of her wages, he reluctantly agreed.

Later that same day, November 5, Theresa Knorr disappeared from her duties as nurse to Alice Sullivan for the entire afternoon, leaving the old lady stranded at a bridge session some distance from her home. Eventually a barman at the bridge club gave her a ride home and a neighbor took pity on Alice—who suffers from Parkinson's disease—when they found her shivering on her cold porch waiting for Theresa to appear with the front-door key.

On Interstate 15, Theresa Knorr had actually been stopped by Utah State Troopers after being spotted weaving in and out of traffic on the busy freeway.

The troopers studied the Utah driver's license: Theresa Jimmy Cross, 1296 North 400 East, Bountiful, Utah 84010. Weight: 170. Eyes: Blu. Birth Date: 03/14/1946. Height: 5ft. 05in. . . .

Minutes later she was arrested on suspicion of drunk driving.

At about 6:00 P.M. that evening Theresa finally turned up back at the house in a taxi, claiming her car had broken down on the freeway.

Incredibly, the woman who was by now the most wanted mother in the entire country was released by Utah law enforcement officials because her maiden name was not on the list of aliases put in the national police-wanted computer.

Pat Thatcher and her brother Bud Sullivan had been very concerned by Theresa's absence, but they believed her excuse about the car breaking down and let things ride because she had been such a loyal nurse and friend to the entire family since starting work there the previous year.

When a group of close family members in from Connecticut turned up at Alice's house for a reunion party the next day, nothing more was mentioned about Theresa's car problems.

At the gathering, Theresa seemed relaxed, sipping sedately from a glass of red wine and laughing and joking with the other guests.

Alice's nephew Thom McMahon was most impressed by his aunt's helper. "When I met her the first time, it was like I'd known her my whole life. She was a very concerned person . . . very friendly, very warm."

But when one of the relatives tried to snap a photo of Theresa Knorr, she slipped conveniently into the background. However, the Thatchers did later manage to get a handful of shots that included Theresa, and she looks the very epitome of a healthy, stable, middle-aged lady.

At the party that Saturday, Theresa made a point of leaving any room each time Pat Thatcher's attractive daughter Shannon walked in.

Shannon—who was in her thirties and married, with three beautiful children—seemed to pose a threat to Theresa Cross.

"Shannon felt that Theresa did not like her from the moment they met. Whenever she visited Alice, Theresa would open the door to her and the kids and then go straight to her bedroom and never reappear until after they had gone. It was almost as if she did not want to share the spotlight with someone prettier and younger than her," recalled Pat.

Old habits die hard . . .

Eighteen

"What kind of mother could do that?
What kind of person am I going to be
throughout my life? That's what I want
to know? How am I going to deal with
it? What's going to happen to me?"

Terry Knorr

On November 6, 1993, Detective Dick Williamson of the Washoe County Sheriff's Department proved to John Fitzgerald that just once in a while cops actually help other cops without needing an ulterior motive. As he promised he would, Williamson had tracked down an address in Reno that he believed to be Theresa Jimmie Knorr's current home.

Fitzgerald and his task force partner Chal DeCecco immediately made a two-hour dash along Interstate 80 to the address. It was a bum lead. No one there knew or had even heard of Theresa Knorr. She may have lived there a few years back, but she had long since gone.

The main problem facing detectives was that Theresa had used a long list of aliases over the years, including all of her married names and a handful of nicknames. From the 1970s they found that she had beaten a bad check rap, and then there were the visits by the Child Protective Services for the alleged child abuse charges she managed to talk her way out of with the same, sweet, guileless charm she displayed on the witness stand in her 1964 murder trial.

In Sacramento, the whole city was suddenly abuzz with news of Theresa Jimmie Knorr's alleged crimes. The *Bee* splashed a headline across its front page that proclaimed: MOTHER SOUGHT IN GRISLY SLAYINGS, TWO DAUGHTERS BURNED, STARVED.

Then, on November 9, Robert Knorr Sr., the father of four of Theresa Knorr's children, decided to go public by agreeing to an interview in the *Bee*. He made it absolutely clear whose side he was on.

"We believe William and we love him and we're behind him a hundred percent," said Knorr Sr. in reference to the charges faced by his twenty-six-year-old son.

He spoke to newsmen outside the Placer County Jail on November 8 after attending a preliminary court hearing for William. Alongside him were his daughter-in-law DeLois and a handful of relatives.

Knorr Sr. blamed his ex-wife for all the problems now faced by his sons, and even assured journalists: "When I left there, I never thought she was really that crazy. But I guess she was. It's a sad story for my children to be treated like this."

Significantly, Robert Knorr Sr. ignored the claims of abuse made against him by Terry. He even claimed that Terry—who has made accusations of molestation against him in her statements to Placer County detectives—was not necessarily his daughter.

"I just went ahead and gave her my name, but there is some doubt in my mind."

Back outside the court, DeLois, who had only ever

known the new law-abiding, clean-living version of William, was close to tears as she said: "We love each other and I'm going to get him home, whatever it takes."

A few minutes earlier, in the neat, ultramodern courtroom, Superior Court Judge J. Richard Couzens announced that William Knorr might not even have been properly charged in an adult court. He ordered that the charges had to be first addressed in Juvenile Court, where a determination would be made as to whether he should be tried as an adult.

William Knorr stood, head bowed, barely able to acknowledge the presence of anyone in that courtroom. His only comment to the judge was that his family were attempting to hire a private attorney, former Justice Court Judge Robert A. Young, to handle his defense. Further proceedings were scheduled for November 23.

On the same day that William was making his first court appearance, Investigator John Fitzgerald got a call from Salt Lake City cops telling them of an address and post office box details for Theresa Cross traced through a driver's license application she had made in Utah three years earlier. They had even managed to locate the make and registration number of a car she had purchased—all thanks to that drunk-driving arrest five days earlier. This time Fitzgerald and Smith were convinced they were close, and they knew they could not leave it to the Salt Lake City police to check out the address.

"It's always better to do these sort of jobs yourself," explained Fitzgerald.

On November 9 they flew on the early evening flight from Sacramento to Salt Lake City.

At 7:30 A.M. the next morning, after a good night's sleep in their motel rooms, Fitzgerald and Smith headed out to the address on South 600 East where they believed Theresa Knorr was living. They had no idea of the circumstances under which she was existing.

When they got to the house, all appeared quiet. The two cars parked outside did not check out as having any connection to Theresa Knorr and since her car was not around, the two investigators decided to return at a later time. They did not want to alert anyone in the neighborhood to their presence, and drove off to the Salt Lake City main post office to see if Theresa Knorr was picking up her mail from the P.O. box she had set up sometime previously.

At the post office, nobody knew what she looked like, and the two detectives considered whether they should just wait and see if she turned up to collect her mail. But that seemed a ludicrous long shot.

"We might have waited a week till she showed up. We did not have that sort of time on our hands," says Fitzgerald.

The two detectives left their cards and a phone number at the SLCPD just in case Theresa Knorr appeared, and then set off to run down some more leads. A forty-five-mile trip south to the city of Provo proved fruitless, and all their other inquiries were equally unhelpful.

At 4:45 P.M., as darkness fell, Smith and Fitzgerald decided to make another run past the house on South 600 East. As they turned right onto Kensington, which ran alongside the corner property, Fitzgerald spotted

Theresa Knorr's red Plymouth, with license plate 083-DBW, parked on the driveway up to the garage.

"Bingo. She's here. She's gotta be," he told his colleague.

The two detectives then headed off for the nearest public phone to call the Salt Lake City Police Department to request an officer to accompany them on the arrest. They were about to detain someone for a crime committed in another state, and there were certain procedures they needed to go through.

Just then a clearly marked SLCPD cruiser drove past them. Fitzgerald swung his small rental car around and within minutes they had managed to wave down Officer J. D. Whitaker, who actually was not even on duty at the time. Under a new SLCPD scheme, he had been allowed to take the patrol car home on the understanding that if any crime occurred while he was in the vehicle, he would automatically go back on duty. SLCPD reckon that the mere presence of police cruisers on the streets can prevent crime. It is an admirable scheme.

Whitaker was at first very cautious. He ran a local check on Theresa Knorr and confirmed that everything Smith and Fitzgerald were telling him was true. The two investigators—while appreciating the young patrolman's reservations—were anxiously watching the time ticking away, fearful that Knorr might leave the house if they did not get back there very rapidly. After some more discussion, Whitaker agreed to accompany the two detectives to the house on South 600 East Street.

Just before 5:15 P.M. the three police officers parked their cars more than a block and a half away from the

Sullivan house just to be on the safe side. They did not want to blow it at this late hour.

Fitzgerald and Whitaker approached the front door of the house while Smith checked out the back. The drapes in the front window were open, and Fitzgerald noticed eighty-six-year-old Alice Sullivan sitting in the front living room, but he could not see any sign of Theresa Knorr. Both investigators were confused by the presence of Alice since they did not even realize that Theresa Knorr was working as a care giver to an elderly lady. Fitzgerald knocked gently, careful not to make it sound like an urgent matter because that might cause the suspect to try and flee. For more than a minute he waited, but there was no reply. He tried again.

Within seconds Theresa Knorr finally answered the door. Fitzgerald hesitated for a moment, before recognizing her from her Utah driver's license photograph. "She looks a lot better than in her California one, 'cause she's fixed herself," he recalled thinking. She had lost weight—about sixty pounds—but she was still short and heavy, she still had short brown hair, and her eyes were still alternately as cold as ice and as warm as the sad, sweet smile she used when she wanted something. Then, out of typical old-fashioned courtesy, Fitzgerald asked her:

"Are you Theresa Cross?"

She did not reply.

"I am a police officer from the state of California and I need to talk with you."

"Not in front of the lady. Come this way."

Theresa Knorr beckoned the two policemen into the house. She was sensitive about the old lady hearing what was happening. Just then, Inspector Smith also appeared and joined them.

Fitzgerald, Smith, and Whitaker followed Knorr to the bedroom at the rear of the house. At this stage none of the policemen had even suggested why they needed to talk to Theresa Knorr. She did tell them she preferred the name Cross to Knorr. "I don't like that name."

Once they got to the back bedroom, Fitzgerald came clean.

"I have a warrant for your arrest on two counts of murder, and we are placing you under arrest."

Theresa looked stunned but said nothing. Then she explained to the officers that she needed to contact the son of Alice Sullivan—the old lady she was looking after—so that arrangements could be made to take care of her.

Fitzgerald allowed her to make the call to Bud Sullivan.

"Bud, it's Theresa here, can you come down to your mother's house," Theresa told him.

Bud knew immediately something was wrong.

"What's the matter?"

"The police are here. They want to arrest me on a warrant."

"What for?"

"I don't know."

Theresa Knorr had too much pride to admit to Bud why she was being arrested.

Then the three police officers and the woman accused of committing two of the most horrendous killings in California history sat down in the kitchen of the house and made polite conversation while they waited twenty minutes for Bud Sullivan to come over and look after his mom.

Fitzgerald believes that Knorr had seen some of the media coverage about the case on the local TV news and was preparing to disappear and reemerge in some other city on the other side of the country.

She was getting ready to flee, but thought she still had a little time. She was going to get a U-Haul, hook it up to her car, go to the storage shed where she kept her other belongings, and then get to the next big city, probably Denver.

Bud Sullivan was still wondering what the problem was as he headed across town with his girlfriend Marji.

"I thought she probably had a bunch of parking tickets. I said to Marji, 'We better post her some bail money so we can get her out to carry on looking after mom,'" he later recalled.

When Bud did finally get to the house, John Fitzgerald took him into a back room and said: "I don't want you to talk to her about this, but she is being arrested on suspicion of murder."

For a moment Bud was stunned. Then he remembered seeing that report about Terry Knorr and her dead sisters on the television a few days earlier. It jogged his memory.

Bud walked back into the kitchen where Theresa was calmly leaning against a sideboard.

"I don't know why they are arresting me," she said. Then silence, followed by an afterthought: "Will you sell my car for me?"

As is sometimes the case with honorable people, the

hunter—in this case Fitzgerald—still had time to sound a little sympathetic toward his prey, Theresa Knorr.

"She was trying to do the best with her life and look more attractive. Wearing nice clothes and all. She wanted to run a clean life and enjoy it without getting involved in any trouble. She did not want to attract any attention to herself," said Fitzgerald.

It sounded a lot like Billy Bob. He had also tried to start fresh . . . until John Fitzgerald came along.

Fitzgerald and Smith decided it wasn't necessary to cuff Theresa Knorr inside the Sullivan house.

Fitzgerald led her outside by the arm and handcuffed her once they were in the front yard.

He put her in the investigators' four-door rental, and SLCPD Patrolman Whitaker followed closely behind.

At 6:20 P.M. Fitzgerald and Smith arrived at the Salt Lake City Police Department with their prisoner. They immediately took her to the interview room on the fifteenth floor, where she was read her Miranda rights by Smith. Theresa Knorr refused to waive those rights and sat in stony silence. The two investigators knew then that Theresa Knorr was not going to be opening her heart up to them for the time being.

"I want a lawyer," was about all she would say.

Within a few minutes Fitzgerald and Smith gave up and decided it was time to leave the room. Fitzgerald went to the door; it was locked. Suddenly it dawned on him that neither he nor Smith had the key, because they were just visiting officers, not actually stationed at the SLCPD.

Theresa Knorr sat stoney-faced at the interview table, unaware of the situation until Fitzgerald started pounding on the door to try and get someone's attention. Two Salt Lake City officers walked past, looked through the glass window and promptly barked at the two California cops: "Get away from there. You'll be let out when the officer gets back."

They thought that Smith and Fitzgerald were prisoners.

"In the middle of all this drama and talk about the appalling crimes this woman was alleged to have committed, we had ended up being prisoners in a police station," recalled Fitzgerald. "It was ridiculous."

As Fitzgerald continued pounding on the door, a sly grin came to the face of Theresa Knorr. It was the only time John Fitzgerald ever noticed her smile.

Eventually they got out of the interview room and escorted their prisoner to the Salt Lake County Jail—the same prison where her daughter Terry had been an inmate after her domestic flare-ups at her in-laws' house. During the four-block drive, Fitzgerald gave Theresa Knorr his business card and said: "If you change your mind, just call me." He wanted to be absolutely certain he had done everything possible to elicit a confession. Theresa Knorr took the card and said nothing. In fact, the only thing she talked about on the way to jail that evening was her three sons, Howard, William, and Robert.

But not once, noted John Fitzgerald a few months later, not once did she mention her daughters.

As they arrived at the jail, Theresa Knorr simply said: "I feel like a sacrificial lamb being led to the slaughter."

The following day was the Veterans Day holiday, so the two Placer County investigators decided they would spend the day following up more leads, trying to contact people who might actually be at home rather than work.

Over at his mother's house on South 600 East, Bud Sullivan was getting a taste of that much mentioned Andy Warhol phenomenon—fifteen minutes of fame. Masses of TV crews, photographers, and reporters had gathered outside the front door for a chat about Theresa Knorr.

Channel 2 proudly reported: "A murderer has been caught right here in Salt Lake City. The suspect: a forty-seven-year-old woman. The victims: her own two children. The case had been a mystery for almost a decade until a surviving daughter gave cops what they were looking for . . ."

Later that day, the hot news was updated to include some footage of the Sullivan house: "Forty-seven-year-old Theresa Knorr is in Salt Lake County Jail. She was arrested in this Salt Lake home yesterday. Knorr is suspected of killing her two daughters nine years ago in California. According to police, her seventeen-year-old daughter's charred body was found in 1984. A year later in Truckee her other daughter was . . ."

In one report, Bud Sullivan—looking distinctly uncomfortable under the glare of the camera lights—said: "It was a complete shock. None of us had any idea about her past."

Bud Sullivan was still having great difficulty believing any of the things he had heard about Theresa Knorr.

One neighbor, Cynthia Russell, talked happily to the TV crews about how her kids used to go over to the house and do odd jobs. "She was a very nice neighbor. My reaction is that they must have the wrong person or something."

Inspector Johnnie Smith—head of the Placer County task force formed to bring the Knorrs to justice—privately admitted in an interview in February 1994 that he was just as surprised by Theresa Knorr as those neighbors.

"I was expecting an entirely different type of person after hearing all those evil things about her. She was more refined, she cared for the elderly, she was respected in the community, people were full of praise for her. No one had a bad word to say about her.

"It was as if she had ended one life to start another. In fact, I think that is what she did. She terminated that evil life and headed for Reno, then Salt Lake."

Reporters even traced Howard Sanders, who, after learning of his mother's arrest, said: "I'm really glad they caught her; I'm relieved. Maybe they can go forward now and find out exactly what went on. Nobody else can be hurt."

At 9:15 A.M. that same morning, Bud Sullivan got a call from Fitzgerald and Smith, who wanted to know how he came to hire Theresa Cross, as she was known to him.

Sullivan admitted, rather embarrassingly, that he had loaned Theresa Cross $4600 after she told him she needed to pay an outstanding tax bill. But he refused to agree with speculation that Theresa Knorr had been planning a long trip somewhere. He believes to this day that she was being pressured for money by somebody.

After speaking to the two detectives, Sullivan went

over to the Salt Lake County Jail to try and see Theresa Knorr. Not only was he concerned about all that money he had loaned her, but he was also genuinely worried about her well-being. He still could not believe the murder allegations.

Bud Sullivan—who had never been near a jail before in his life—discovered the logistics of prison visiting are not as simple as one might imagine. Theresa's other good friend, Hal Cheney, had already been contacted by her and made a visit at noon that day. Prisoners were only allowed one visit per day.

Cheney—another clean-living character who had no previous experiences of the Salt Lake prison system— had gotten off to a bad start when he turned up at the jail's imposing entrance to be told there was no Theresa Cross in custody.

"But we have got a Theresa Knorr," the prison warden informed him.

A few minutes later he walked into the stark visitors' room and watched through the glass partition as he waited for Theresa to appear. When she did walk out of a side door, Cheney was taken aback by seeing her in prison tunic and wearing little makeup. She looked very different from the charming, quietly confident lady he and his wife Fran had known for more than three years.

He hesitated, then picked up the phone to talk to his friend on the other side of the glass screen.

"I want you to know that I am innocent of the charges against me," she told the pensioner before he had even uttered a word.

"I don't even know what the charges against you are," replied a bemused Hal Cheney.

"I am charged with two counts of murder."

For a moment there was silence. Cheney was visibly shocked by Theresa's admission. He tried to say something more to her, but it was so difficult to know what to talk about after that.

"Is there anything I can do for you?" he finally asked her.

"I could do with a toothbrush, some toothpaste. Those sort of things."

Hal Cheney left Theresa a twenty-dollar bill and walked out of the visitors' room of the jail. He saw Theresa two more times, leaving a twenty-dollar bill at the end of each visit. But he later admitted—in an interview in February 1994—that "we never talked much. Just sort of sat and stared at each other."

Theresa Cross called Hal Cheney from jail a few days later and told him: "You don't really miss your freedom until you have lost it."

Later that first week of her detention, Theresa Knorr got a visit from her old friend at night school, Keith Bendixen. He arrived at the Salt Lake County Jail with a stack of religious books, only to be told he could not take any into the prison, in case he was hiding something in them to help her escape with. Keith had an awkward fifteen-minute visit and has not seen Theresa since.

On November 12, just before his departure back to California, John Fitzgerald visited the jail and asked Theresa Knorr if she would waive her extradition rights. She refused to and calmly told the investigator she had some things she wanted to take care of in Utah and had no intention of leaving if she could help it.

At Placer County Jail, on hearing of his mother's arrest, William Knorr met with task force member Chal DeCecco and insisted that his mother had admitted murdering her first husband and been involved in the death of her sister, Rosemary Norris, even though detectives had already discounted such suggestions.

Nineteen

The most insidious effect of abuse is
that it dramatically increases the
likelihood that the victim-child will
become a victim-spouse or worse, a
child abuser.
Paul Mones, Author

At 10:00 A.M. on that same Veterans Day holiday,
John Fitzgerald spoke to David Lundberg at the Sandy
Police Department to see if he had come up with any
record of Terry having told the police previously of her
sisters' killings. Lundberg told Fitzgerald about all
those domestic violence calls from the house on Pepperwood where Terry lived with her in-laws, and how he
had confronted one of his fellow officers in Sandy.

At 10:30 A.M. Fitzgerald contacted Terry at the house
in Sandy and tried to get some more specific details on
those earlier occasions when she told the police about
what had happened inside the Knorr household. She
mentioned telling a sheriff who came over to her friend
Heidi Sorenson's home, and she gave Fitzgerald the
names of seven other people she had told over the
years.

Fitzgerald was very concerned about these alleged
earlier reports, and headed over to the Bountiful Po-

lice Department at 12:15 P.M. lunchtime to try and track down some concrete evidence of Terry's claims. All they could come up with was an address for Heidi Sorenson on West Center Road. Fitzgerald went straight over there, but no one was in, so he left his business card and a note asking her to contact him, that it was urgent.

The following day, Fitzgerald went to the house in Bountiful where Theresa Knorr had worked before moving to Alice Sullivan's place. He was trying to fit as many pieces of the jigsaw together before he had to fly back to Sacramento.

Fitzgerald was fascinated by the way Theresa Knorr had changed her entire life after moving to Salt Lake City. Everywhere he went, people talked in glowing terms about her. It was as if she had reinvented herself.

It took Fitzgerald another three days of digging to uncover which cop Terry had spoken to when she met Heidi's friend the sheriff three years earlier. He located Woods Cross Police Department Chief Paul Howard and discovered that the report had been made by Clarence Montgomery. Fitzgerald then tracked down the name of the detective in Sacramento who handled the inquiry.

Meanwhile, Theresa Knorr continued to fight extradition back to California. That meant Smith and Fitzgerald would have to go back to Sacramento without their star defendant.

The *Sacramento Bee*—still following the investigation closely—ran a story on November 13 that rubbed disappointment into John Fitzgerald's wounds:

WOMAN CHALLENGING EXTRADITION IN DEATHS OF 2
DAUGHTERS

Placer County sheriff's detectives returned empty-
handed from Salt Lake City on Friday after learning
that the woman charged with the murders of two
daughters will challenge authorities' attempts to return her to California. . . .

The following Monday, Theresa Jimmie Cross—
charged in the torture slayings of two of her daughters
—was formally arraigned when she appeared before the
Third Circuit Court in Salt Lake City. She was ordered
to be held without bail.

At the Placer County Jail, in California, William
Knorr was scheduled to face a fitness hearing in the
local juvenile court to decide whether he should be
tried as an adult for his alleged crimes. He had been
sixteen when Suesan was killed and seventeen at the
time of Sheila's death.

Since the murderous antics of Ma Barker and her son
Fred in the thirties, through the weird, sick killings by
the creepy McCrarys, in Texas, to the sexually depraved
California orgies of death committed by Gerald and
Charlene Gallego, America has always loved families
that allegedly commit heinous crimes. And now, in middle-aged Theresa Jimmie Knorr, it had the suspected
ring leader in the flesh! Within days of the news of her
arrest leaking out, Theresa Knorr's story and photograph became front-page news across the world.

First, big profile coverage came in the prestigious *Los
Angeles Times* on November 14. In a lengthy front-page

piece headlined 'UNBELIEVABLE' TALE REVEALS GRISLY CRIMES, the paper reported all the details, peppered with quotes like, "I have been here 33 years and I have never seen such a bizarre case" from Placer County Sheriff Donald J. Nunes.

Nationally syndicated talk-show host Sally Jessy Raphael requested interviews with the defendants and Terry. They were soon followed by *America's Most Wanted, Inside Edition.* Then came *USA Today*, the Associated Press, and the *New York Times*, to name but a few.

In Placer County, Sheriff Don Nunes was juggling calls from CBS in New York and ABC in Washington. "It is unbelievable, but it is understandable because of the savage behavior involved. It's the motherhood aspect that has caused all this coast-to-coast interest," the sheriff told one pressman.

Fierce competition between the news media—which the sheriff described as "frothing at the mouth over this story"—had caused Nunes to back off and take a conservative approach. To avoid any facts from being misconstrued, Nunes insisted all news media queries were responded to by prepared statements.

"If Sally Jessy Raphael wants to come out here to talk, that's fine, but all legal questions will be referred to the district attorney," he warned the ladies and gentlemen of the press.

Everyone, it seemed, wanted to talk to Terry Groves, the one surviving daughter who had finally brought her mother's alleged crimes to the attention of authorities. KUTV's scoop in getting Terry in front of the cameras a few days earlier had undoubtedly been influenced by her own determination to remind authorities that now that things were out in the open, she did not want her mother escaping justice.

Now the whole world was requesting interviews with the brave daughter who had the courage to keep going back until someone listened.

Even the tabloids—who usually ignore the most grisly crime stories in favor of celebrity tittle-tattle—got on the bandwagon. *Globe* headlines screamed: AMERICA'S MOST EVIL MOTHER. Accompanying the article was a photo of Theresa taken from her Utah driver's license, complete with painted-on prison bars just to get the message over loud and clear to *Globe* readers.

Detective David Lundberg at the Sandy Police Department—who had bonded so well with Terry during the previous few weeks—found himself inundated with calls from journalists, screenwriters, and Hollywood producers, all desperate for Terry's home phone number. He called her up and told her of all this interest, and she begged him not to tell any of them what her married last name was, let alone where she lived.

"I don't want to talk to anyone. You just screen all the calls for me," pleaded Terry to her policeman friend.

So it was that Detective David Lundberg—eleven-year vet of the Sandy Police Department—became, in his own words, Terry Groves's agent. It was an unusual move on the part of the young detective. Police officers do not often work as show-business representatives for witnesses in major murder investigations. But he explained: "Terry wanted to get the story out, but she wanted it to go out in a proper way, without exploiting the death of her sisters. She also wanted to sell it for money. I was acting, and I hate to use this term, but I was acting, so to speak, like an agent for her."

He soon found himself screening dozens of calls every day from aggressive Hollywood types, all desperate to sign up the rights to the Knorr story. Agent Lundberg dismissed all of them as being very untrustworthy, until Joe Dipasquale, of Quest Entertainment, came along.

"I had no experience, but I basically had to use my gut instinct, and I felt comfortable with this guy. He sounded very straightforward."

On the Sunday morning before Thanksgiving, Terry Groves put on her one and only dress and escorted her husband Mike, her attorney, and Detective David Lundberg to the Little America Motel, in downtown Salt Lake City, to meet Hollywood producer Joe Dipasquale. It was a controversial move on the part of both Terry and her policeman-turned-agent. Not surprisingly, the entire meeting was kept very quiet and not a word about it was ever revealed to the media at the time.

Dipasquale went over the contracts as the group sat in his suite. Terry asked a few questions about what writers the producer was planning to use and how the movie would be treated. Dipasquale reassured her it would be done very sensitively, and then she signed the contract.

A few minutes later the happy group were enjoying a slap-up brunch at one of the city's best restaurants.

"Let's celebrate with champagne," announced Terry just before they started the meal. She ordered a bottle of Moet & Chandon and they made a toast. By signing that contract with Joe Dipasquale, Terry had just earned herself more money than in her entire working life—and it was all thanks to the alleged horrors inflicted inside the Knorr household. Agent David Lundberg also cosigned the same deal with the Hollywood producer. It is not known precisely how much he will earn from the eventual television movie of this extraordinary story.

But officers with the Placer County task force are not so impressed. Inspector Johnnie Smith would only say of Lundberg's involvement: "I don't know how legal it is."

On December 9, Theresa Knorr launched an all-out bid to prevent herself from ever being extradited to Placer County, California. She appeared before a Third Circuit Court commissioner, who stayed extradition proceedings after learning that her court-appointed lawyer had filed a petition seeking a writ of habeas corpus.

An indignant Theresa Cross—as she was now referred to—still insisted she was innocent of all the charges against her.

She claimed she was not in California at the times of her daughters' deaths, and accused authorities in Utah and California of not having followed correct extradition procedures.

Theresa Cross's publicly appointed defender, Paul Quinlan, even conceded after the hearing that he was trying to buy time for his client—time to let the media hysteria in California and the rest of the world die down.

Quinlan knew full well that extradition warrants could only be attacked on limited fronts. Cross had three possible defenses: she was not a fugitive because she was not in California when the crimes occurred; she was not the correct person being sought; or, the court paperwork had a technical glitch.

County Prosecutor Bud Ellett said he expected to file a response to Theresa Cross's writ by the following week, and he warned that one of the Placer County task force investigators might be called to testify at the hearing. But court officials predicted at least a two-week delay on the extradition hearing.

Despite this setback, Ellett assured newsmen at the court that he still believed she would be deported. It was just a question of time.

In Placer County, task force investigators tried to play down their disappointment by saying: "Most of the evidence is pretty much intact. We've waited ten years. We can wait a little longer."

In Auburn, California, William Knorr's attorney, Michael Brady—retained by DeLois Knorr for her husband—asked Placer County Judge J. Richard Couzens to delay his client's arraignment until December 20. Brady said he wanted the extradition hearing in Utah to be completed first because he felt that William Knorr should be tried jointly with his mother. He also wanted to give attorneys time to research the question of the Knorr brothers being juveniles at the time of the alleged killings and how that would affect their eventual trial. Judge Couzens also appointed respected Auburn attorney Mark Berg to represent Robert Wallace Knorr, still in prison in Nevada for that unrelated murder.

Berg told the court: "My client may have been under sixteen at the time and there's some question about whether the district attorney can even prosecute them after all these years."

Berg also insisted that the arrest warrant that was issued by the adult court might not be valid because of the age problem.

Luckily, Placer County investigator John Fitzgerald had a mole inside the Salt Lake City Police Department who kept him informed of every development as it occurred. Fitzgerald's pal, detective Marv Hammer, called him at Tahoe City to tell him the latest news.

"I've got a feeling that the judge is going to throw out her request at the next hearing," Hammer told Fitzgerald. He promised his colleague in California that he would go to the hearing the next day and contact him as soon as he heard the judge's decision.

"Then you can come and get her before her attorneys file for any more delays," promised Marv Hammer.

The following morning, Fitzgerald was pacing up and down his small office awaiting the all-important call. He had in his hand a written authorization, personally signed by Pete Wilson, Governor of California, which empowered him to take fugitive from justice Theresa Knorr into his custody and then back to California. He also had a similar order from the Utah State Governor. The paperwork was all in, now he just needed his prisoner. Fitzgerald had even brought his packed overnight bag with him into work especially. At 10:30 A.M., Hammer came on the phone.

"You're on. The judge denied her request and she's free to go. The only stipulation is that you must bring a female officer with you."

In Salt Lake City a devastated Theresa Cross had made a last desperate appeal to the judge by claiming that she could not fly because she suffered from sinus problems. The judge was not impressed. "It won't hurt you" was his only response.

At the Tahoe City substation, Fitzgerald called Sheriff Don Nunes, who approved the trip to Salt Lake without hesitation and told his staff to book the investigator plus woman detective Laurie Ziegler on the next flight to Salt Lake City.

Fitzgerald and Ziegler checked into a motel in the center of Salt Lake City, had a bite to eat, and then called Marv Hammer to make arrangements to meet them at the Salt Lake County Jailhouse at nine next morning. Hammer made a call to the prison to ensure that the two detectives could get in without any last minute problems over jurisdiction. Fitzgerald also insisted that Theresa Cross should not be told about the specific plans to extradite her until eight next morning —just in case she got her attorney to try more blocking tactics.

But Theresa Cross knew her departure for California was imminent. She just didn't know exactly when she would have to leave, so she put in a collect call to Alice Sullivan's son Bud and told him that she needed to hire another attorney to avoid extradition and could he advance her $500.

"Theresa, I've advanced you everything I am going to," came Bud Sullivan's terse reply.

Theresa Cross still insisted to Bud Sullivan that the $4600 he had loaned her the previous week had all been paid off toward her taxes. But Sullivan had been in touch with his bank and knew the check he gave Theresa had been cashed the day he loaned her the money. She must have been lying.

That last call to Bud Sullivan was the turning point for Theresa Cross. In her cell at the Salt Lake County Jail that evening, she meticulously drew a brightly colored Christmas card for her close friends, Bud's sister Pat and her husband Vere.

The card consisted of three candles sparkling brightly with some holly below them on a piece of rough prison-issue paper. On the left side she had written, "Merry Christmas and a Happy New Year."

On the opposite side she wrote a message to her friends saying she was leaving for California and thanking them. "Friends are as precious as fine gold," wrote Theresa. She wished them a happy Christmas and signed off by saying: "My thoughts are with all of you. Love Theresa."

John Fitzgerald walked into Theresa Cross's prison cell at just before nine the next morning. She did not utter one word. Fitzgerald cuffed her unceremoniously with handcuffs that went around her waist and wrists and told her:

"There won't be any problems just as long as you don't cause me any problems. Our job is to transport you from Utah to California, and if you just do as we ask, then it'll all be okay. You treat us decent, we'll treat you decent."

Fitzgerald meant every word. Here was a classic opportunity to humiliate his notorious prisoner, but he preferred to allow her to keep some dignity.

At Salt Lake City Airport, Fitzgerald was relieved to see there was absolutely no sign of the expected media circus to greet them. Just before they got to the check-in area, he allowed her to hide her manacles under a small red coat. Then Fitzgerald, his prisoner—complete with that red coat, a floral blouse, and black pants—and Detective Ziegler found a quiet corner by the departure gate and waited for boarding to be announced.

After fifteen minutes Fitzgerald spotted, to his horror, a crowd of TV crews and reporters swarming up the corridor like a pack of hungry, noisy hyenas.

"There she is."

"That must be her."

They had been tipped off about that distinctive red coat. This time Theresa Cross was the one with nowhere to escape. She looked petrified. Even Fitzgerald felt a flush of anger. He just wanted to get his prisoner home to Auburn with the minimum of fuss and attention.

"We understand you are going to give us an interview," one brazen reporter assured John Fitzgerald. He was appalled that anyone should try to trick him so overtly.

"No way," was about the politest Fitzgerald could be in the circumstances.

Just then the flight was called. Fitzgerald and Laurie Ziegler grabbed Theresa Cross by the arms and tried to march her through the waiting newshounds. Flashbulbs popped, but the crowd made way. One look at Fitzgerald's stern, determined expression told them not to push their luck.

Once on board, John Fitzgerald sat down with Theresa Cross between him and Ziegler. They made some pleasant, civilized small talk as the jetliner soared up out of the Salt Lake Valley and headed for California.

The conversation stayed mainly on an impersonal level.

Theresa Knorr talked about Utah being a very nice place to live, that there were good people there and how the Mormons were very considerate.

But one particular comment by his prisoner stuck in John Fitzgerald's mind.

"People in Utah treat women much better than they do in California," said Theresa Cross. She should know . . .

Fifteen minutes before landing at Sacramento Airport, Theresa Cross told her two police escorts she wanted to go to the rest room. Fitzgerald undid her cuffs and escorted the sizable Cross as she waddled down the aisle toward the toilets. Before letting her in the cramped compartment, he checked it for any razor blades or other items that might have been left in there by previous occupants.

"Okay. In you go, and don't forget to unlock the door the moment we knock on it," explained Fitzgerald.

Theresa Cross squeezed into the toilet with just a tatty plastic bag containing her purse and a few items of makeup.

After four or five minutes, Fitzgerald and Ziegler

looked at their watches anxiously and began to wonder why she had still not emerged. Fitzgerald calmly headed back down the aisle and knocked on the little door.

Theresa Cross emerged almost a completely different person from just a few minutes earlier. She was perfectly made-up and had neatly brushed her hair. She looked almost glamorous, a bit like Roseanne Arnold's mother perhaps.

"There was a twisted vanity about her. Her appearance was always very important to her. She always tried to look good whatever the circumstances," commented John Fitzgerald.

Theresa Cross had just spent five minutes ensuring that she would look her best when the plane landed and she found herself under the media spotlight. She wanted to be certain she would look as good if not better than everyone else. But it was all a delusion . . .

Twenty

> In ancient times, when might was right, the infant had no rights until the right to live was ritually bestowed. Until then the infant was a nonentity and could be disposed of with as little compunction as for an aborted fetus.
>
> Samuel Radbill, author of *The Battered Child*

Placer County Sheriff Donald J. Nunes is the kind of guy who doesn't do things by halves. He also knows a good press opportunity when he sees it, and the arrival at Sacramento Airport of the by-now notorious Theresa Knorr on a Delta Airlines flight from Salt Lake City on December 18, 1993, promised to be a classic media event.

John Fitzgerald—sitting in his window seat as the plane taxied to its terminal—was hoping, praying, that they could get her down the steps and out of that airport with the minimum of attention. As the plane came to a halt, he saw Sheriff Nunes standing below him on the tarmac with the reassuring sight of four Placer County officers. The sheriff had even brought along his own dark blue Chrysler New Yorker to whisk the threesome away as quickly as possible. Then Fitzgerald saw at least fifty members of the press, angling their cameras directly at the aircraft. There would be no easy escape.

As Fitzgerald, his prisoner, and colleague Laurie Ziegler emerged at the top of the aircraft steps, the whirl of motor drives made Theresa Knorr's homecoming seem more like a presidential visit than the arrival of a woman alleged to be one of the most evil mothers of all time.

Once on the tarmac, Fitzgerald ignored the barrage of questioning and pushed Theresa Knorr and Ziegler in the backseat of the Chrysler before getting in front with the sheriff. Theresa Knorr looked terrified and said nothing.

But the press circus had only just gotten into gear. As the Chrysler screeched around the main terminal, journalists started chasing the car on foot. Every time the sheriff's car slowed down on the trafficky airport tarmac, a few healthy reporters caught up and tried to thrust their notebooks and microphones in the window. There was also another problem for the law officers—they could not leave the airport until they picked up Fitzgerald's Explorer, parked on the lot next to the main runway.

After circling around three more times and successfully wearing out even the fittest journalists, Sheriff Nunes pulled alongside Fitzgerald's car in the parking lot, and Ziegler, Fitzgerald, and Theresa Knorr swapped vehicles hurriedly and headed off on the forty-minute drive to the Placer County Jailhouse at Auburn.

The area now called Placer County was home to the peaceful Southern Maidu Indians for hundreds of years before the discovery of gold in 1848 brought hordes of miners from the East Coast.

Just three years after that, Placer County was formed from portions of Sutter and Yuba counties. It took its name from the Spanish word for sand or gravel deposits containing gold. Miners washed away the gravel, leaving the heavier gold, in a process known as "placer mining." The city of Auburn became county seat after being settled by a French gold prospector called Claude Chana, who turned it into a shipping and supply center for hundreds of gold camps.

According to some rather eccentric local folklore, Auburn got its name when, at an outdoor meeting of Indians, one Indian was dancing around an open fire, fell down and burned his hands. When he got up, he exclaimed: *"Ah burn."* It sounds an unlikely tale. Tourist guides these days describe the city as "a wonderful example of Sierra foothills living at its best."

Placer County's 1431 square miles encompass a variety of terrains including everything from flat grasslands through rolling foothills to the Sierra Nevada Mountains. The population in 1985 was 135,300, including a significantly low racial mix; 1.5 percent Asians, 7 percent Hispanic, less than one percent black, and one percent Native American.

But it was the construction of Theresa Knorr's favorite Interstate 80 more than a quarter of a century ago that opened up Placer County and led to more than a third of its employed residents traveling to and from the California state capital of Sacramento.

The people of Auburn still remember another notorious case, that one involving children alleged to have murdered, which occurred just before the tragic death of Suesan Knorr.

On June 14, 1983, Anna Brackett, age eighty-five, was waiting for her son's visit when two girls knocked at her door and asked for a drink of water. Usually wary of strangers hanging around her quiet condominium complex in Auburn, Anna felt no fear when she agreed to let Shirley Katherine Wolf, fourteen, and Cindy Lee Collier, fifteen, into her home. After all, they were only kids . . .

One hour later Anna was found dead, lying in a pool of blood, stabbed twenty-eight times with a knife from her own kitchen. Police questioned neighbors and local youth authorities, and early the next day found the two runaways hiding in Cindy's house. Confessing to their grisly crime, Wolf and Collier were arrested and one month later tried by a Superior Court judge without a jury. They were sentenced to the maximum penalty under the law: to be kept in a California Youth Authority correctional facility until they reached the age of twenty-seven. It later emerged that both girls had suffered from family neglect and hideous sexual abuse that had robbed them of their childhoods and drove them to kill.

The brief Auburn winter, for which no one was ever quite prepared, arrived early the morning after Theresa Knorr's dramatic return to California. A bitter breeze flowed west from the Sierra Nevada Mountains, and in the great American tradition of public buildings in winter, it was so hot in the Placer County Courthouse, you felt trapped inside your clothes and there was nothing to breathe except thick steam heat.

First to be led into the immaculate, beige-colored courtroom was Theresa Knorr, handcuffed and wearing ill-fitting regulation Placer County inmates' tunic and pants in her favorite bright red.

The six television cameras, two still photographers, a radio reporter, and two newspaper photographers allowed in the court recorded every move.

Theresa Knorr sat down opposite Judge J. Richard Couzens, the huge seal of the state of California between them. The stars and stripes were to the judge's right, the bear of the California state flag to his left.

No sooner had Theresa Knorr sat down on the brand-new maroon-colored seat than her son William was brought in by two uniformed guards. They guided him alongside his mother. Neither looked each other in the eye. She kept her eyes set on the beige carpet. His eyes snapped around the room nervously.

William was terrified about sitting next to his mother. He had turned over a new leaf once he left his mother's home. Suddenly, that previous life had reemerged and threatened his future. He looked pale and scared.

Then ex-husband Robert Knorr Sr. got up and screamed at Theresa Knorr.

"I hope you burn in hell for what you did to my kids, woman!"

The whole court stopped. Knorr Sr. glared. Reporters watched excitedly.

Theresa Knorr glanced in the direction of her ex-husband and gave him a cool stare. It was a look that seemed to say: "I am still in charge."

Later Knorr Sr. claimed, as if to defend his actions, that he had reconciled with his son William and had been regularly visiting him in jail since his arrest. He said that his son was innocent and very depressed about the charges.

But his father's outburst in court that morning simply had the effect of making William Knorr look even more terrified. He leaned over and whispered a few words in the ear of his attorney. Seconds later William Knorr was moved away from his mother to a row behind her.

In the public gallery, the assembled media watched in fascination because they knew that this was the first time mother and son had seen each other since those alleged crimes were committed inside that house just off Auburn Boulevard all those years earlier. Cameras continued to click. This was a photo opportunity none of them wanted to miss.

Theresa Knorr tried desperately to use her attorney to shield herself from the family members and the press in the public gallery just ten feet away. She could feel the hatred emanating from her ex-husband, Robert Knorr Sr., DeLois Knorr, the daughter-in-law she had never met before, and a handful of friends who had come to court.

The press pack scribbled furiously. None of them was going to leave the steaming courtroom until every last detail of this first appearance of mother and son had been squeezed out.

A few minutes later the attorney agreed to a continuance and the case was adjourned. Theresa and William Knorr were solemnly led away back to their cells.

William Knorr's attorney Michael Brady said afterward that he hoped all future court appearances could be arranged so that mother and son were not in sight of each other. "My client is distraught about being in court with her."

Ironically, Brady also told newsmen after the court appearance that although William Knorr wanted no part of being around his mother, he still felt it was best to keep the two defendants linked in court.

"If it is true that she was an overbearing mother, I want them tried together because she is responsible for the alleged homicide, not my client," said Brady.

At the Placer County Jailhouse attached to the courtroom, Theresa Knorr and her son William each occupied eight-by-ten cells in the part of the prison given over to solitary confinement for punitive or protective reasons. This was a high profile case, and the protagonists of such dramas are often considered vulnerable to starstruck inmates happy to grab some glory by attacking notorious defendants.

Neither Theresa Knorr nor her son were particularly comfortable about their enforced incarceration, and—although men and women inmates have been openly mixed inside Placer County's modern, air-conditioned facility since it opened in 1988—they avoided each other like the plague. Weak, yellow-orange lights burned in both their cells most of the night, which was fine if you were an insomniac with plenty of books to read, but very distracting if you were not. The cells had a bed, a toilet, a sink, even a tiny desk balanced on lockers. In Theresa's, she had a three-inch window looking out onto a pond in a picturesque field at the back of the jail. Sometimes she watched pheasants hopping and skipping across the pastures as a few geese swam lazily back and forth in the pond. On another occasion, an orange-and-white-striped cat stalked a dove in the same field while a bluebird whistled in a small pine tree close by. On January 22, Theresa Knorr was allowed a rare treat—a walk in the grounds. She also became a prolific letter writer and, from the day she arrived in Auburn, scribbled away furiously to all her friends back in Salt Lake City.

In his cell on the other side of the facility, William Knorr was allowed to work out in the weight room and then shower. The rest of the time he did pushups and situps. Both Knorrs were allowed to make collect telephone calls. But neither saw any newspapers or watched television. Jail rapidly started to become a way of life for them.

In Salt Lake City, many of those close friends of Theresa Cross, as she called herself in that city, were still reeling from the shock of her arrest and extradition to California.

Pat Thatcher, the daughter of Alice Sullivan, and her brother Bud Sullivan, had the unenviable task of boxing up all Theresa Cross's belongings and storing them away just in case she ever got back to collect them.

They carefully stacked her jewelry, makeup, and books in cardboard boxes and then took all her clothes out of the closet in that porch area where Bud had built a rail to take all Theresa's extra clothing. They also dismantled a treadmill she had gone to great lengths to have delivered to the house, although it was rarely used by overweight Theresa.

Just as Pat was removing the last of Theresa Cross's dozens of pairs of one-inch-heeled pumps, she noticed a number of carefully wrapped gifts stacked neatly in the corner of the closet. The mother who allegedly had inflicted so much pain and suffering on her children had been looking forward to another friendly family Christmas in the Sullivan household and had already bought at least half a dozen gifts to give her new family.

"It was so sad. I took them down to the basement close to tears. I still cannot believe that a good person like Theresa could be responsible for the crimes she is accused of," Pat said recently.

And Bud Sullivan still stoutly defends Theresa Cross, despite the fact she tried to trick him into lending her yet more money the night before her extradition to California.

"Maybe Theresa is protecting her kids and does not want to implicate the others and that's why she's saying nothing. Maybe she was not involved in what they say. Who knows?" Bud said.

Twenty-one

> From victims in the home, they go on
> to become victims and victimizers on
> the street.
> Paul Mones, Author

Every day, investigators gathered at the task force headquarters at Inspector Johnnie Smith's office in the Placer County Sheriff's Office in Auburn. On the walls were maps of the region, as well as photos of Suesan and Sheila, their mother and two brothers. Bagged-up evidence—jewelry, clothing, makeup—still lay strewn on Smith's desk.

The detectives' job was prodigious. But the investigation could have been even more complicated if Sheriff Nunes and his officers had not taken full responsibility for both deaths, despite the jurisdiction problems.

John Fitzgerald knew full well that Theresa Knorr's much publicized arrest did not mark a slowing down of the investigation process. On the contrary, he had to keep pushing for nugget after nugget of information that would contribute to her eventual trial on murder charges alongside her two sons.

His main aim was to interview as many of the other Knorr family members and friends as possible. The task force was particularly interested in Knorr's oldest son,

Howard Sanders. On November 16, Investigators Smith and DeCecco reinterviewed him to clear up a few loose ends from his earlier statement, on November 3. They were especially interested in establishing exactly how Howard came to be informed of his sisters' fate. Sanders was fully cooperative, and no suggestion has ever been made that he was in any way involved in the deaths of his sisters.

Howard Sanders's wife Connie also provided a fascinating insight into life inside the Knorr household, including colorful references to black magic. She had also witnessed some of the abuse inflicted on the Knorr daughters.

Other important developments included the discovery of William Knorr's palm print on the popcorn-cup box that Sheila's crunched up corpse was dumped in. Bonnie Paolini, latent print examiner at the California Department of Justice, must take credit for that and the later matching of two of William Knorr's fingerprints and one of his brother Robert's on a plastic bag found near the spot where Suesan died.

Meanwhile, brief court appearances at the Placer County Courthouse became Theresa and William Knorr's only glimpse of the outside world.

On the day I visited the court, Monday, January 31, 1994, it was a crisp, sunny, fifty-degree winter day, with a cool wind cutting through from the mountains to the east.

The first thing anyone inside the courtroom noticed was the fidgeting, gray-haired man sitting in the aisle behind me. He wore a shapeless suit and tie, not really in keeping with the man himself. His face was stern, steel-edged, but unemotional, almost devoid of expression. He looked dead ahead of him without blinking once. A slight belly bulged through his white shirt. That was Robert Wallace Knorr Sr., the father of four of Theresa's children.

And there was a sizable cast of other characters there too.

DeLois Knorr, William's wife, glowered uneasily from the front row after acknowledging the presence of her father-in-law. William Hall, longtime friend and car pool associate of William Knorr, looked on with concern. Another pal of William's was Nikolaas Bos. Both men later insisted their good friend was completely innocent of the charges. In the front row, a local TV newsman had set up his camera on a huge tripod, ready to get some fresh footage of mother and son the moment they appeared. At least a dozen other journalists, print and TV, filled the remaining rows of seats.

Just then, the expectant courtroom quieted down.

Theresa Knorr, unemotional, wrists cuffed at the front, was led into the hushed room from a door at the back of the court. Investigators told me before the court hearing that she had lost at least fifty pounds, thanks to the diet inside jail. Her face seemed sallow; the skin beneath her chin hung almost like a turkey's. The prison clothes, still her favorite crimson-red, did not help. Her hair parted down the middle and frizzled from lack of conditioner. As cameras clicked in her direction, she seemed momentarily flustered. There was even a flicker of anger in her eyes. She was led to a chair at a table. She seemed relieved when her court-appointed attorney, Mickey Sampson, appeared alongside her. From that moment on she played a game of cat and mouse with the waiting pressmen and family members by ensuring that Sampson blocked their view of her.

William Knorr, head bowed, was led in through the same wooden door as his mother a minute earlier. His wrists were cuffed at the front, his face pale in contrast to his bright, crisp, and clean orange prison clothes. William walked to the middle row of seats well away from his mother and sat down, not looking up for even a second, in case he caught the eyes of the waiting family, friends, and media . . . and worst of all, his mother, who sat just three feet in front of him.

Judge J. Richard Couzens referred to her as "Miss Cross" throughout the brief hearing. Neither mother nor son were required to utter a word, but her attorney, Sampson, made an interesting request to the judge. Center stage at last, Mickey Sampson, in his mid-thirties, had a soft, dark beard, shaped so the round white baby jowls and soft chin didn't show. His longish, well-groomed, brown hair shining despite the onset of baldness, Sampson wore an inoffensive brown suit and had a friendly but somewhat anxious demeanor.

"We object strongly to her not being allowed to wear her own clothes," the public defender said. "We ask that the order be lifted for her next court appearance so that Miss Cross be allowed to wear civilian clothes."

The Honorable J. Richard Couzens denied the request and announced that June 14, 1994, would be the date of the case arraignment. Theresa Cross's vanity had outlasted two secret lives and the murder charges hanging over her head . . .

Twenty-two

> And hope does not disappoint us,
> because God has proved out his love
> into our hearts by the Holy Spirit
> whom he has given us.
> *Romans* 5 (New Testament)

In her friendless cell at the Placer County Jailhouse in Auburn, Theresa Cross was feeling lonely, confused, but still determined, no matter what, to keep in touch with friends from Salt Lake City.

On January 12, 1994, Alice Sullivan's daughter got a moving letter from Theresa, which reduced her and her one-time tough cop husband to tears. She referred to "how hard all this is on my friends. My attorney said I will find out just who my real friends are."

She insisted that just because her children were saying things, that they were not true. Theresa Knorr called her arrest and the charges "a holocaust" and thanked her friends for standing by her in her "darkest hours." She even described her three-inch-wide cell window which overlooked a pond across the street and a little of the field below. She signed the letter: "Love in Christ, Theresa."

"It hardly seems the sort of letter a hardened criminal would write, does it?" Pat said after reading it.

"Whatever happens to Theresa, she will always have a friend in us."

On the same day, January 12, Theresa Cross's other good friends, Hal and Fran Cheney, got a letter from her that offers yet more insight into her state of mind as she awaited her trial. In it she quoted Romans 5, from the New Testament: "And hope does not disappoint us, because God has proved out his love into our hearts by the Holy Spirit whom he has given us." She said she read scriptures every day and had no one to talk to except the Lord our God.

Theresa Knorr also revealed that the jail chaplain had given her a new international version of the Bible and she had just finished reading the great lion of God, about Saul of Shish, which she found inspirational. She also read *Heaven and Earth*, about a Jew and a Catholic in the 1930s in Canada. She signed off "In Christ Love, Theresa."

Just two weeks later Theresa wrote another lengthy letter to Fran and Hal Cheney. Fran could hardly contain her emotion about her good friend Theresa and wept as she read this letter, written in blunt pencil. It referred to how twenty quails and six Canadian geese had flown over and decided to land on the pond outside her cell window. Seeing the geese made her realize how much she missed her freedom. She also came to appreciate the "little things," like having tea and a piece of fresh fruit.

The Cheneys were so touched by the letter that they wrote back to Theresa promising they would come and see her at the Placer County Jail on their next trip to California. They have also received a number of collect telephone calls from her since her extradition to California.

Meanwhile, at the Sullivan house where Theresa Cross was arrested on November 10, 1993, there is one lasting memory of the woman who devoted herself to looking after eighty-six-year-old Alice Sullivan. Still parked up in the driveway to the neat, suburban one-story house is Theresa's pride and joy, her 1986 Dodge, colored her favorite crimson-red, naturally.

April 1994

As of this writing, Theresa Jimmie Cross and her son William Robert Knorr are still being held in protective custody at the Placer County Jail in Auburn. Both mother and son are watched closely by corrections officers.

In jail, Theresa Cross continues writing vast numbers of letters, while William reads books. He frequently makes collect phone calls to his wife DeLois, and occasionally to his father, Robert Knorr Sr.

At the Nevada State Prison, in Ely, Robert Wallace Knorr is still refusing to cooperate with investigators, and it is expected that he will be brought to Placer County to face the charges concerning his sisters' deaths before the next major hearing, in June 1994.

In Salt Lake City, Terry Knorr—her mother's only surviving daughter—found that the pressures of living under the same roof as her in-laws plus the worldwide publicity surrounding her allegations put an enormous strain on her marriage to Mike Groves. In February 1994 she reluctantly parted from her husband and moved back to the Sacramento area. Once again, mother and daughter found themselves living just a short distance apart, yet neither had any compulsion to meet.

The actual trial of Theresa Knorr and her two sons will probably happen sometime in the early part of 1995, when the painstaking process of choosing a jury will begin.

Meanwhile, Theresa Knorr meets frequently with her attorney, Mickey Sampson, currently mapping out a defense strategy. He will no doubt try to suppress any statements she made to investigators just after her arrest. The attorney will argue that without a full videotaped confession or a written account of the alleged crimes, his client should also not be held to statements made by individuals who might also be implicated in the killings.

An insanity plea may well be considered if she confesses to the killings. But it will only be accepted after a rigorous fight. To be acquitted under such a plea, the defense has to prove that at the time of each murder, the suspect was suffering from a mental illness or defect, and failed to know or appreciate that what she was doing was morally wrong.

Prosecutors want to ensure that Theresa Knorr and her two sons are found guilty and never go free. They will likely fight an insanity defense by calling psychiatrists to testify that all three knew precisely that what they were doing was wrong, and call into evidence the fact that the crimes were covered up after they were committed. They will point out that Theresa Knorr and her sons methodically planned the murders and disposal of the bodies, and that they tried to conceal their connections to Sheila and Suesan by removing all evidence of actual identification.

There is absolutely no doubt that Theresa Knorr's only surviving daughter, Terry, will play the most crucial role in the outcome of the case. Her key testimony about life inside the Knorr household and the deaths of her sisters is expected to keep the court riveted for days.

Then there is Mark Berg, attorney for William Knorr. He is still insisting that Placer County has no business prosecuting the notorious case because their home was in Sacramento at the time of the alleged killings.

"It is shocking that Placer County would attempt to prosecute a case where the victims and the defendants are from Sacramento," says Berg. He intends to continue challenging the territorial jurisdiction issue because one of the homicides has no connection to Placer County.

Berg claims the jurisdiction issue has been caused by investigative evidence that shows Sheila Sanders died in the closet at the family apartment in Sacramento. He also noted that her body was found in an area fifteen feet inside the Nevada County side of the Placer-Nevada county line. Berg observed that state law allows any county to prosecute as long as elements of the crime occurred in the prosecuting county. "But there is no connection with Sheila's death to Placer County," said Berg, insisting that either Nevada or Sacramento counties—not Placer—had the right to prosecute.

"Whoever made the decision to burden Placer County taxpayers with this case acted irresponsibly," added Berg, who estimates it will cost hundreds of thousands of dollars, if not millions, to prosecute Theresa Knorr and her two sons.

Placer County District Attorney Paul K. Richardson was reluctant to discuss the merits of the case. "It would behoove me to wait and see what [Berg] is going to file. We think we are on good ground to prosecute the case in Placer County," he said.

Berg did at least acknowledge that Placer County had jurisdiction to prosecute for the death of Suesan. But he also pointed out that Sacramento County had jurisdiction in Suesan's death as well because the defendants allegedly planned her death while at home in Sacramento. He is pushing for the two homicides to be dealt with together in one trial, in Sacramento.

Richardson admitted that his office had been in conversation with representatives of the Sacramento District Attorney's Office on the case, but he would not elaborate or confirm that Sacramento District Attorney Steve White had agreed to let Placer County handle both cases.

Berg also said that he believes Placer County Deputy District Attorney Dan Dong will try to justify doing the Sanders homicide in Auburn because the defendants drove through Placer County while taking her body to its dumping spot in the Tahoe-Truckee area.

But, said Berg, transporting the dead girl's body through the county line does not justify having Placer County take over the prosecution. Berg warned that he intended to file the motion to challenge territorial jurisdiction as soon as his client, Robert Knorr, makes an appearance in the Placer County court.

* * *

As the legal system presses ahead with its case against Theresa Knorr and her two sons, John Fitzgerald and the rest of the Knorr task force will continue their investigations. They are still hunting for more clues to the killings, and continue to be stunned that with each breakthrough come yet more astonishing claims about life inside the Knorr household.

California's Department of Justice continues to examine the items found near both bodies in the hope that yet more evidence will be linked to the defendants. They will be looking for traces of blood, hair, fingerprints, even carpet fibers that might help confirm the awful events surrounding the killings of Sheila and Suesan.

Whoever uncovers the complete truth about this remarkable case, there seems little doubt that, if proven guilty, Theresa Jimmie Cross and her two sons will go down in history as one of the most gruesome families of killers in modern times.

There have been few instances where family members have actually started systematically murdering their own loved ones in cold blood. One of the few cases that comes to mind is that of so-called stepmother from hell Sueanne Hobson. In May 1982 she was found guilty of engineering the killing of her husband's only son.

Hobson had seemed like the ideal wife: vivacious and attractive, flawlessly organized, the devoted mother of a pretty young daughter from a previous marriage. And she had willingly accepted the troubled past of her new husband, Ed Hobson—a past of horrifying, inexplicable tragedy. Then the nightmare erupted that shattered the unity and destroyed the hopes of the Hobson family forever. On a quiet spring evening in the sleepy mid-western town where they lived, Chris Hobson, Sue-anne's stepson, was driven to a remote rural area and shot dead while lying inside the grave he had just dug.

Charged with murder were Sueanne's formerly es-tranged seventeen-year-old son, James Crumm Jr., and his high school buddy, Paul Sorrentino. Crumm fin-gered another, especially unlikely accomplice: his mother, Sueanne. Her crime: hiring Crumm and Sor-rentino to carry out the shotgun slaying because, she allegedly said, young Chris was causing too much trou-ble at home. Unsure of her innocence, Sueanne's hus-band Ed divorced her. Then, in a change of heart, he remarried her, and now he remains devoted to his im-prisoned wife, the woman convicted of killing his only son.

But there was one big difference between the Sue-anne Hobson case and the allegations facing Theresa Jimmie Cross and her two sons: the Knorrs killed their own flesh and blood, according to the one surviving sis-ter, Terry Groves.

Twenty-three

"Everyone has the capacity to kill."
Forensic psychiatrist Peter Wood

A crucial part of Theresa Knorr's defense strategy will be an extensive evaluation of her medical condition at the time she was alleged to have killed both her daughters. Forensic psychiatrists and psychologists have already begun to interview her at the Placer County Jail.

These "mind experts" are called into every major homicide case soon after the arrest of a suspect. Their modus operandi is to initially interview the subject, having deliberately done the minimum of research on the case. Often nothing more than a newspaper clipping is read in advance of that first meeting because the mind experts prefer to hear a full account of a suspect's alleged crime in his or her words with their own interpretation of exactly what happened. That alone helps the psychiatrist or psychologist during initial evaluation of a crime.

After that first interview is concluded, the mind experts begin a painstaking research process that includes collecting information from a vast range of sources including relatives, medical notes, school reports, comments from employers, and witness statements for both defense and prosecution. Notes that police have collected about a subject's background can also often prove useful.

If the defendant has got a psychiatric history, then notes and even a general practitioner's comments are obtained. Then there follows a series of much more intense interviews with the subject.

It is vital here to outline the major differences between forensic psychologists and psychiatrists because there tends to be a good deal of overlap between the two professions. The psychologist is not usually medically qualified, having studied pure psychology and the development of the mind. The clinical psychologist judges a subject, based on his or her abnormalities, and is trained to carry out a certain range of checks that require a practicing certificate. Part of that investigative process is in forensic work. However, a forensic psychiatrist is not qualified to give those same tests. They require a specific form of training and usually come from a general medical background and then go on to specialize in psychiatry. They alone are empowered to prescribe drugs for people.

The most important single factor when it comes to the role of psychiatrist or psychologist is to evaluate whether someone is different from the average man in the street. What changed them? And are they capable of doing it again?

Forensic psychiatrist Dr. Peter Wood is one of the world's foremost experts in what drives people to kill, having worked on more than 400 death-related cases over the past fifteen years. He says: "There isn't a correlation between severity of offenses and mental problems. You can be very normal and kill someone. Naturally, I have a familiarity with the territory, but one must never get away from the shock horror of somebody who has killed someone else. To detach from the emotion that people feel about homicide is quite natural in my profession. But, by the same token it is very important not to get out of step with the way people in general feel about murder. Otherwise you become too blasé about it."

Even after that first interview with a defendant, the mind expert will rough out a report on a suspect. They will have gone to great lengths to ensure that the subject interviewed did not get distressed. After all, that first meeting is a starting point for what will eventually be formally written up for the actual trial. The mind expert sets up a series of questions for the defendant. A lot of the time it is remarkably easy to tell if someone is of normal intelligence or not.

Often there are clear indications. The difficult cases are the ones where somebody has done something inexplicable and they themselves seem totally ordinary. Certainly there are elements of this in the Knorr family despite the problems that exist in the background of many family members.

The key questions that will be asked at the eventual Knorr trial will be: What was in their minds when the alleged crimes were committed? What motivated the offenses? The experts will want to recreate every step taken by the defendants in an effort to repeat the events exactly as they occurred, so that a full picture of the initial killings can be properly revealed. Experts now believe such careful analysis not only assists an ongoing trial, but can help avoid future tragedies.

Criminal psychiatrists are convinced some groups of people will almost definitely reoffend. These are the ones where great care and attention must be paid when considering an application for an early release from a custodial sentence.

The system for careful mental analysis of defendants has become an integral part of the justice system over the past twenty years. As a result, the cases of repeat homicides is getting lower. The one exception to the rule is that there are still a lot of people who kill children, are then imprisoned, only to get released and commit similar offenses again.

Undoubtedly, where the victim is a child, there is a greater risk of repetition. The average sentence served for child homicide or manslaughter in many so-called civilized countries like the U.S. is less than ten years. Usually it is men in their early twenties who commit many of these offenses. By the time they are in their early thirties, many of them have killed a child, served a sentence, gotten out again, and are at an age when, by definition, they are going to be in a position where they could be around young children once more.

There has also been a disturbing increase in the number of teenage women who become involved in murder in similar circumstances as young males. The instances of random, nonpremeditated killings committed by young women has been growing faster than it has in young men.

One of the most extraordinary statistics about female

killers is that more than half of those serving sentences for murder haven't struck a blow.

Dr. Wood has his own theories as to why: "I put it down to the manipulative skills of women, who—although it may seem sexist of me—seem capable of getting men to commit their crimes for them." An interesting comment when considering the prosecution case against Theresa Knorr and her two sons.

On the whole, women still mainly kill for revenge. If the prosecution's case is proven, Dr. Wood believes that part of Theresa Knorr's motivation may have been that she was aware of the alleged molestation between her husband Robert Knorr Sr. and his daughter, and that turned her into a vengeful woman.

At first, her evil intentions might, more understandably, have been directed toward her husband because of the abuse he inflicted on her children. But when he left home, her resentment—and probably jealousy—was turned inward to her own daughters, who in her eyes had "stolen" the physical love of her husband and "deprived" her of her marital rights. In a twisted way, in the mind of his wife those daughters became the equivalent of Robert Knorr Sr.'s mistresses—and she began to harbor increasing resentment toward them.

If this scenario is true, it seems that Robert Knorr Sr. was fortunate not to have been physically harmed. There have been many cases in recent years where sex offenders have been cut down by vengeful women.

Recently, in England, a woman was acquitted on the basis of lack of intent despite the fact she killed her own stepfather because she suspected he had sexually interfered with her own daughter. She told the jury she intended to stab him in the penis and testicles. She wanted him to suffer untold agonies.

It was his word against hers. He had earlier been charged with molestation, but the case had been thrown out for lack of evidence. Explained Dr. Wood: "She obviously felt very stressed by that."

One of Dr. Wood's most recent cases featured a female babysitter, just eleven, who killed a child in her care. The case left Wood with a clear impression of what drives children—especially teenagers—to kill.

"There are usually serious things wrong in their own childhood," he explained. "They failed to learn how to limit their behavior because of their own experiences. A child often has to become totally amoral in order to survive. If you have to fight your way through childhood because you are being mistreated, you don't grow up with the right limitations on your own behavior."

Sometimes, the defendants will even try to put a romantic glow on their childhood when in fact they had a very miserable time.

"A lot of people will say, 'Well, my father used to belt me but I deserved it,'" explained Dr. Wood. "Then I would say, 'What did you have to do to get belted?' And they would say, 'If I was late home from school and had dirty knees.' I would say, 'Isn't that a little excessive?' And they would say, 'Maybe.'"

One of the biggest problems facing the Knorr defendants—besides the obvious seriousness of the charges they are facing—is the public outcry that followed their arrest in late 1993. That response of shock and horror that a mother and her sons could allegedly cut down their own flesh and blood is a very human reaction, but it has sparked fears for the safety of those defendants.

As one senior investigator involved in the Knorr case explained: "When people are accused of such awful crimes, there is a real danger that someone might try to get even with them."

In jail, the Knorrs are kept in solitary confinement because of concerns over their safety from inside and outside those prison walls.

However, many mind experts like Dr. Peter Wood look on the accused in some domestic homicides as the "victim." A classic example is the wife who kills an abusive husband after being driven to it by his violence. It will be interesting to see how Theresa Knorr's defenders handle such aspects.

In such cases, psychologists say that undoubtedly the guilt—even if it is not apparent in many defendants—will continue to haunt the accused for the rest of their lives.

Dr. Wood added: "In a way, the abusive husband who died has the last laugh, because these women do not tend to walk off into the sunset with a new man on their arm. Most of them are haunted, broken victims."

Frequently, abused wives who have faced years of physical and sexual torment at the hands of brutal husbands or lovers, kill in the heat of the moment while trying to protect their children from a beating. Many such wives are devastated by their actions afterward and frequently glorify the memory of their bullying husband—something that often leads to a gross miscarriage of justice.

The biggest single common denominator among some of the most notorious killers in recent years has been their extraordinary ability to create a so-called "mask of sanity."

In other words, the accused's dark and sinister behavior is often masked by a veneer of very good and socially rewarding activities. This mask has, according to experts like Dr. Joel Norris—Ph.D. in psychology and a founder member of the International Committee of Neuroscientists to Study Episodic Aggression—manifested itself through grandiosity or a belief in their own superhuman importance, hypervigilance or an extraordinary concern about acting morally and properly, and social adeptness to the point of extreme manipulative ability.

Many defendants in episodic killings demonstrate the basic attributes of an effective manager (or parent). "The ability to get other people to do what you want them to do," explained Dr. Norris. Many are strangely capable of sensing the inferiority in others, the need to be dominated and told what to do, and the desperate need for approval. Those under the spell of such people tend to appear on the outside to be normal, upstanding males and/or females, albeit with free spirits. But actually they are more often than not deeply scarred people who actively seek domination as a missing component in their own personalities.

By possessing that keen sense of what is required to conform to the outward trappings of society, people who kill others are often able to exhibit acceptable, indeed exemplary, behavior in their own communities.

"Their need for approval and their ability to second-guess confrontation is so great that they go undetected by the public at large," Dr. Norris added.

The qualities that compel people to carry out episodic killings are eerily similar to those qualities that American society expects from successful individuals. They often see themselves as "doing good," having penetrated the very society they hated so much.

But there is one part of the personality of such killers that remains in all of us—the need to be accepted and the will to achieve. In the case of the accused, there can be no actual satisfying or satiating it, whereas normally developed people can decide when to be "selfish" and preserve quality time for themselves. Dr. Norris and other experts say that virtually all such killers have little or no self-esteem—psychobiologically, many of them cannot determine the boundaries of their own selves and thus cannot conceive of themselves as having separate identities—and this is the factor that contributes to their eventual explosion of violence.

This means that most of them have spent a lifetime repressing the cancerous rage at the core of their personalities. A progressive and escalating loss of control and sense of madness becomes apparent to them from the time they first become aware of their own dark, primal urges. Such people learn to hate and fear their own evil side, yet cannot help but succumb to it in moments of pure reactive violence. However, they often develop a chameleonlike mask of sanity or normalcy whose purpose is to protect them from the turbulent and hostile violent central element of their psyches. This mask of sanity also camouflages them from the society they have learned to fear and hate.

During this period in an episodic killer's development, a unique set of mechanisms emerges, composed of the same elements that make for sociopathy or sociopathic and multiple personalities, and these interact with the neurological impairments that cause significant but convenient losses of memory and gaps in reality: the episodes during which the series killings are committed. "The drive to live within society, the ability to hope and dream about the possibilities the future holds for them, and the sense of self that allows them to benefit from personal and vocational achievements, have all been physically or emotionally beaten away from them in their earlier years," explained Dr. Norris, providing an eerie insight into the background of such killers.

Another characteristic of such episodic killers is that they become pathological liars. On the one hand, lying is simply an extension of chameleonlike ability to blend in with their background. They sense the information that people around them want to hear, and provide it. "Truth is not an issue for them," Dr. Norris explained. "Survival is."

Truth also demands that a person perceive a modicum of self-worth. Because most episodically violent individuals see themselves as having no real worth and no meaning for life, they are honest neither with themselves nor with others. On a practical level, say the experts, lying is a form of manipulation. If one can lie successfully, one can get others to believe what one wants them to. But when lying becomes chronic in the schoolchild or in the person whose recapitulation of basic facts may change from day to day, it is a clear indicator of other serious behavioral disorders. Dr. Norris believes that most episodic killers sincerely believe the stories they are telling when they are telling them.

Twenty-four

> The violent act becomes necessary as a
> means of asserting the will and
> compensating for real or imagined
> humiliation.
> Brian Masters, Author

This brings us to Theresa Knorr's own background. Mind experts will want to delve into her family history before she met and fell in love with her first husband. They will probe her own childhood for evidence of incidents that might help to explain her later actions as a mother. The chances are that she herself was either molested or sexually abused as a child. Her parents' attitudes toward crucial elements of her upbringing, like sex, money, and love, will also have shaped her later domestic problems. Undoubtedly, the premature death of Theresa Knorr's mother will be considered as a significant turning point in her childhood.

In some other recent episodic killing cases, the death of a parent or grandparent has been cited by mind experts as a possible cause of resentment that gradually built up into a crescendo of horrific violence. Dennis Nilsen—Britain's most infamous serial killer, with a tally of sixteen young male victims—was shaken by the death of his beloved grandfather when he was just twelve years old. Psychologists insisted after his trial that Nilsen's obsession with death was fueled by the sight of his grandfather lying in an open coffin before his burial.

Only in the past few years have professionals begun to understand the process through which such ultimately malevolent individuals have been created in each generation. These so-called experts are now coming to appreciate how such episodic violence is shaped by patterns of child abuse, pathologically negative parenting, brain injuries resulting from physical traumas, inherited neurological disorders, chronic malnutrition, chronic drug and alcohol abuse, and even toxic poisoning from environmental pollutants.

There is a very common cycle of deprivation that involves the repetition of often similar offenses a generation later or sometimes even two generations later. Public health officials even concede that such cycles of violence in all their various forms have been spawned from previous generations. "Parents who abuse their children, physically as well as psychologically, install in them an almost instinctive reliance upon violence as a first resort to any challenge," Dr. Joel Norris said. "Each generation teaches the next generation to react with violence, often reinforced and compounded by the media. Those patterns of violent behavior spread, consuming increasingly greater numbers of victims."

Dr. Norris is particularly critical of the way that, until recently, episodic killers tended to be treated as either sociopaths or psychopaths and were immediately relegated to the care of the criminal justice system. "They are treated as though they were within the range of normal human existence, yet had willingly become deviant," explained Dr. Norris. "But this is not the case. They are nonpersonality types who eventually come alive only during the episodic cycle of murder. However, because the criminal justice system concentrates on apprehension and punishment, rather than on discovering the causality of violence and preventing its spread, individuals who display this type of medical syndrome have slid through the system untreated."

Dr. Norris believes that this lack of·understanding has directly helped increase the number of killers in our midst. "The infection has been allowed to spread through society like a plague: the emerging killers are the carriers, transmitting the syndrome from one generation to the next."

The Knorr case presents an extraordinary opportunity for criminal experts to examine in minute detail the background and circumstances of a series of killings that is unique in its very nature because of the close family ties between the victims and their alleged killers.

In the eyes of many, Theresa Knorr and her two sons should qualify as serial killers if found guilty of the charges they face in the deaths of Suesan and Sheila. The term "serial killer" usually refers to criminals who do not kill their victims simultaneously. In other words, there is a period of time between each death.

This is not to be confused with the description "repeater," which is used when referring to criminals jailed following the killing of one victim and then released from prison only to murder again.

Criminologists across the globe will be watching the

Knorr case closely. As acknowledged U.S. expert on murder Marvin Wolfgang said: "Homicide can be 'caused' by practically any type of major psychiatric illness." World-famous forensic psychiatrist Dr. Peter Wood is particularly intrigued by the case: "It is extraordinary in itself that she allegedly killed her own flesh and blood. But to be apparently a joint serial killer with her two sons is even more unusual." Dr. Wood, from England, has investigated the minds of many killers over the years and gained a unique insight into their minds. But even he is stunned by the alleged circumstances behind the deaths of Suesan and Sheila.

After some careful consideration of the facts behind the case, he concluded: "The mother who kills her children when they are older is likely to be either schizophrenic or paranoid psychotic."

Dr. Wood believes that the most significant allegation concerning the crimes that Theresa Knorr is said to have committed is that she apparently managed to kill twice—and on separate occasions—and did it with two of her own sons.

"That makes her less likely to be psychotic because she has involved others. If you are driven by delusion, unless you draw someone else into your own delusions, the motive for killing is foreign to the person you are trying to involve in your behavior. Almost by definition, people who kill jointly are not psychotic. That's the simplest way of putting it."

One of the most astonishing aspects of the case—whatever the outcome—is that it took so many years for Theresa Knorr and her sons to be brought to justice. Terry Knorr's efforts to alert authorities to the killings have already been well-documented in this book, but there is another aspect that has so far been overlooked —the inability of police to come up with any profile of the killer of the two girls, even though it was clear they had both been unlawfully killed (although authorities had not linked the deaths at that time).

Many criminologists believe that too much emphasis is being put on profiling killers. Often, some insist, these profiles prove wholly—or certainly partially—inaccurate. In the case of both Sheila and Suesan, no actual profiles were produced because investigators believed they did not have enough clues to build up a picture of the girls' killers. They were also unaware of their family connection.

Privately, police in Placer County say that was the precise reason why so little action was taken initially to track down the killers. For over the past two decades, investigators have become so used to using profiles to help bring killers to justice that when no such "picture" exists, many police inquiries rapidly fizzle out.

Since the deaths of Suesan and Sheila ten years ago, police homicide units have become far more sophisticated in their investigations and tracking of killers. Detectives tended to be strictly reactive up until recently. When a murder was reported, investigators gathered what evidence they could, traced the victim's identity, and tried to reconstruct the crime from what they could determine about the victim's movements during his or her final hours. If there were witnesses, they were interviewed also. But this procedure fails miserably when dealing with episodic, apparently motiveless killings. The reason for this is simple: such crimes do not fit into any set pattern. The motive for murder is not dependent upon the particular situation or upon the individual victim. In this case, without an identity or any clues as to the allegedly domestic nature of the girls' deaths, police were left with next to nothing.

The truth of the matter is that reactive homicide investigations depend upon things like weight of evidence, clues at the crime scene, relationship between victim and the murderer, involved witnesses or passersby, and, finally, the fear and guilt of the killer him- or herself. In the case of Suesan and Sheila, the police were virtually empty-handed.

Yet, the chilling facts of the matter are that, since 1980, more than twenty-five percent of all murders in the United States have been "stranger" homicides in which the killer is not driven by any apparent rational motive, and since detectives looking into the deaths of the two girls did not even have their identities, they could not link the killings with anyone. Investigators naturally find such cases frustrating because the killer may be in the area for only a short time before disappearing. Worse still, in rural areas like the Sierra Nevada Mountains, there are the added problems of jurisdictions that do not routinely share information about unsolved homicides. The alleged killers of Suesan and Sheila were never even the target of a combined task force, until after Terry Knorr had finally persuaded investigators to act upon her claims.

At the time of both girls' deaths, detectives only had a crime scene as evidence. They had absolutely nothing else to go on until after the autopsies, and even those medical examinations did not provide many additional clues other than incidentals which proved fruitless to investigators. They also faced further investigatory problems because both girls died—or were near to death—in a different location from where they were eventually dumped. This created, in effect, two crime scenes, and caused added confusion to the detectives until they began a piece by piece search of the homes where the girls had lived. But again, this was *after* Terry's story had finally been believed. Interestingly, many experts believe that the killer who strikes first and then takes the bodies to a remote location is less in control.

Another factor that undoubtedly helped the alleged killers of Suesan and Sheila avoid detection for so long was the lack of publicity the girls' deaths attracted. Front page news in local newspapers was hardly enough to raise any real interest outside of the immediate communities where their corpses were discovered. In retrospect, the lack of any real press and TV coverage for those killings helped keep the police efforts out of the spotlight, and arguably, if the case had received more publicity, then someone farther afield might have recognized the descriptions of the bodies and done something about it. Further, it should be pointed out that although family members recall seeing small mentions of the killings at the time, more extensive coverage might have prompted them to react more positively.

Detectives have also speculated that the killers of the two girls found it easy to put the murders into the back of their minds because there were so few reminders of their crimes in the newspaper and on the television.

What is important about the profile of a killer from a

policeman's point of view is that it's impossible to see a complete picture of the criminal's motivation until well after he or she has been apprehended and diagnosed. Current police training still focuses on the traditional murderer who is not compelled to murder and who flees because he fears the police and prosecution. Often the episodic killer will go on committing enough crimes to ensure his own destruction. What made the alleged killers of Suesan and Sheila so difficult to apprehend was that they stopped killing.

One senior homicide detective summed it up by saying: "The breaks usually only come by chance." Another crucial aspect of the initial police investigation is whether the killer or killers were confident enough to spend time at the crime scene, or whether they felt the need to leave it immediately after killing and/or dumping the body. Again, the evidence to police in the Sierras was minimal. They really were up against it. There were no significant clues forthcoming.

Dr. Peter Wood, whose experiences with killers put him at the forefront of such expert knowledge, has dealt with a number of cases that contained relevant aspects to the case of defendants Theresa Knorr and her two sons.

The most similar was one of his patients who killed her ten- and twelve-year-old daughters together in cold blood in the north of England some years ago. The woman was diagnosed as depressed, and she'd been treated for depression before her feelings of resentment toward her daughters manifested themselves into the tragic killings.

Initially, she tried to feed her daughters a lethal cocktail of drugs and alcohol to snuff out their young lives. But when that failed, she bludgeoned and stabbed them to death in the front room of their family's tiny terraced home after she had sent her unsuspecting husband out to get a birthday cake for one of the little girl's birthdays.

The woman was proclaimed a paranoid schizophrenic. Afterward she admitted to Dr. Wood that she would have killed her husband if she could have found him—a significant statement when one considers the obvious hatred that existed between Theresa Knorr and Robert Knorr Sr.

There are also indications that Theresa Knorr was suffering from delusions at the time she and her children were living together in Sacramento. Some of the incidents recalled—in police statements—by her relatives and friends reveal apparent paranoia.

But the woman killer treated by Dr. Wood differed from Knorr in one crucial way. She was deeply depressed by the awful deaths she inflicted on her daughters, and attempted suicide shortly after their deaths. There is no evidence at the time of writing that Theresa Knorr was similarly affected by the deaths of her own flesh and blood.

But, just like Theresa Knorr, this woman was also completely wrapped up in her own feelings and thoughts. Knorr's self-imposed seclusion inside the family's house for weeks on end appears to be clear evidence of her inverted state at the time.

Dr. Wood spent many months gently coaxing his patient to confess her true motives for ending the lives of her own children. It may well be that the forensic experts lining up to interview Theresa Knorr will find similar problems in extracting information about her true feelings. Knorr's life in Salt Lake City following the deaths of her daughters clearly indicates that she had neatly compartmentalized the killings so that they would not rest constantly on her conscience. Everyone who encountered her in Utah got the impression that she was in complete denial about the horrendous crimes she allegedly committed.

Another interesting parallel between Dr. Wood's case and the Knorr charges was that the psychiatrist's patient became—just as Theresa Knorr apparently did—completely paranoid about her neighbors. She felt that people in the street were constantly spying on her, running her down and criticizing her for the way she looked after her children. Those similarities between the two cases make chilling reading.

Following the departure of Robert Knorr Sr., Theresa Knorr's loving care and attention for her children completely broke down. It was as if she had developed an overwhelming sense of responsibility for all the family, and her way of getting out of that was to abuse those people she was responsible for.

Most violence in the family is perpetrated by parents against their children. Researchers have established there are three basic categories of violence against children.

1. Ordinary violence: hitting and slapping is by far the largest category—approximately ninety-seven percent of all children are struck at least once a year.

2. Severe violence: almost nine million youngsters in the United States between the ages of three and seventeen are victims of assaultive acts which go beyond pushing, slapping, and throwing things and which therefore carry a high risk of causing injury serious enough to require medical attention, that is, kicking, punching, beating up, stabbing, and shooting.
3. Then there is very serious violence, when lasting injury and sometimes even death is inflicted.

Yet, despite all the facts and figures and horror stories, society persists in its idealization of the family as an island of peace in a savage, chaotic world. Incidents of family violence are drastically underreported, while accounts of violence perpetrated by strangers continue to find their way into banner headlines.

Though society's refusal to acknowledge and begin to deal with the gruesome reality of family violence seems perplexing on the surface, it is not difficult given the family's sacrosanct importance to society. No one doubts that the exercise of strong parental authority, especially in a child's formative years, is essential to healthy, normal development. Consequently, however, parents wield an unparalleled degree of influence and power over their children, who are completely dependent upon them.

Only recently has society openly admitted that some parents abuse that sacred power entrusted to them. It wasn't until 1984 that the federal government formally recognized family violence as a critical social problem by creating the Attorney General's Task Force on Family Violence. Notwithstanding these strides in recognition and changes in policy, the parental prerogative remains protected in many ways, a distinct double standard for judging victims and perpetrators of child abuse that still exists throughout society today. Paul Mones, a respected U.S. lawyer who specializes in defending children who kill, explained: "This double standard is evident in our social attitudes and in the legal system."

Dr. Wood's case in the north of England bears another uncanny similarity to the tragedy of the Knorrs. The city where this once loving mother came from is gray and industrial, just like Sacramento's sprawling satellite towns where Theresa Knorr and her clan lived.

In both cases there appears to have been a very slow and gradual buildup to the killings. There is also a definite suggestion that it was a very calculating process.

The mother in the north of England even tried to get hold of a gun, because that would have enabled her to kill her own husband later. But purchasing firearms in Britain is much more difficult than in the United States and she failed to find a weapon. No one but Theresa Knorr knows if she harbored thoughts of ending the life of her one-time husband, Robert Knorr Sr. After all, twenty years earlier, she had escaped a jail sentence, despite killing her first husband.

But perhaps the most remarkable aspect of Dr. Wood's case is that the killer mother has now been released from a mental hospital following a conviction for manslaughter—due to diminished responsibility. She has even moved back into the same house with her husband. He has been warned that one day her paranoia may reach another crescendo, and if it does then he could become her next victim. Yet, for the time being the couple appear happily married once more. The husband insists he is so in love with his wife, he will take whatever risks necessary to remain married to the woman who killed their children.

"It was a question of sitting down with the husband and saying these are the warning signs because you are next in line," explained Dr. Wood. (At the time of writing, husband and wife are still living relatively happily together.)

Dr. Wood says that it is very significant that in the case of the Knorrs, a number of family members allegedly colluded in their crimes. "They did not blow the whistle on each other," he explained, "and they found a remote spot to dump the bodies." His interpretation? That they were trying to make sure their crimes remained hidden forever.

Dr. Wood believes that it is possible that Theresa Knorr's first husband—who died at her hands—was unfaithful to her and that sparked her seething hatred.

Another of Theresa Knorr's problems may have been motherhood at such an early age. Many experts believe that teenage mothers are much more likely to batter their children because they are emotionally immature and unable to cope with many of the everyday stresses and strains of motherhood.

Baby battering itself reached almost epidemic proportions in the early to mid-seventies, when Theresa Knorr was bringing up her children, often singlehandedly. Constantly under pressure from lack of money— and frequently without an adult male in the household —the family unit was disintegrating in front of her very eyes. Then there were the regular moves from one community to the next, leaving mother and children little opportunity to establish themselves or their lives with new friends.

Talking to a psychiatrist can often be far less traumatic than talking to the police, and it is entirely possible that Theresa Knorr will reveal more about her alleged crimes and background through such meetings. The mind experts tend to cover the same ground as the official investigators, but in a different way.

Whatever happens to Theresa Knorr and her two sons, tragically, there seems little doubt that the system will not follow through with extensive medical help after the trial in 1995. Often it is left to the discretion (and kindness) of a psychiatrist or psychologist to provide free help because defendants such as the Knorrs cannot afford the high cost of medical treatment. Most mind experts believe that subjects like Theresa Knorr should continue seeing them for at least *ten years* after a conviction or acquittal. It remains to be seen what, if anything, can be done to help answer the dozens of so far unanswered questions surrounding virtually every aspect of this astonishing case.

Postscript

It would be reassuring to believe that murder was a gross abnormality, a dramatic departure from respected ethical standards that restrain civilized man from surrendering to his basic instincts. Once, murder was considered to be beyond the pale, irreconcilable with the rest of mankind. But now, advances made in our knowledge of ethology, evolution, and human psychology present challenges to such banal assumptions which cannot be ignored. Unfortunately, as man has become more civilized, intelligent, creative, and dominant, he has also become more murderous.

Statistically, murder is still rare in proportion to the population. So the type of crimes allegedly committed by Theresa Jimmie Knorr and her two sons are even more baffling, as they fall into three categories: domestic, episodic, but seemingly random (although this later turned out not to be the case).

Murder is a purposeful deed which, by horrid paradox, enables a murderer to reach previously nonexistent levels of violence. Yet that very act often makes him or her despicable to the rest of us, but renders him healthy and admirable in his or her own eyes.

Author Brian Masters studied in great depth the motivation of notorious British serial killer Dennis Nilson, and he concluded: "It is hardly surprising that the murderer is reluctant to show remorse for his (or her) acts. It would be a retrograde step, a kind of psychological suicide . . ."

About the Author

WENSLEY CLARKSON was one of Britain's most successful young journalists before moving to Los Angeles with his wife and their four children in 1991—an experience that inspired his book, *A Year in La La Land*. His other books—which have sold in more than a dozen countries —include the tabloid newspaper exposé *Dog Eat Dog*, a biography of the actor Mel Gibson, plus four best-selling true-crime books *Hell Hath No Fury*, *Like A Woman Scorned*, *Love You to Death Darling*, and *Doctors of Death*.

"AN INVALUABLE BOOK FOR ANYONE WHO WANTS TO UNDERSTAND SERIAL MURDER."

—Joseph Wambaugh

WHOEVER FIGHTS MONSTERS

My Twenty Years Tracking Serial Killers for the FBI

ROBERT K. RESSLER & TOM SHACHTMAN

He coined the phrase "serial killer", he advised Thomas Harris on *The Silence of the Lambs,* he has gone where no else has dared to go: inside the minds of the 20th century's most prolific serial killers. From Charles Manson to Edmund Kemper, follow former FBI agent Robert K. Ressler's ingenious trail from the scene of the crime to the brain of a killer in this fascinating true crime classic.

"THE REAL THING. ABSOLUTELY MESMERIZING."

—Ann Rule, author of *Small Sacrifices*

AVAILABLE WHEREVER BOOKS ARE SOLD
FROM ST. MARTIN'S PAPERBACKS

SHE LOVED HER SONS...TO DEATH.

Hush Little Babies

THE TRUE STORY OF A MOTHER
WHO MURDERED HER CHILDREN

DON DAVIS

Not since the Susan Smith case has a murder so
shocked the nation: a beautiful, loving mother is
horrified to find her two young sons stabbed to
death on her living room floor by an intruder.
Hearts go out to poor Darlie Routier, who appeared
to live for her children. But overwhelming evidence soon finds Darlie, the neighborhood's "Most
Wonderful Mom," guilty of slaying her own innocent
children in cold blood . . .

**AVAILABLE WHEREVER BOOKS ARE SOLD
FROM ST. MARTIN'S PAPERBACKS**

HUSH 11/97

A HANDSOME OVERACHIEVER AND A BEAUTIFUL
HONORS STUDENT MADE THE ULTIMATE LOVE PACT...
MURDER.

BLIND LOVE

THE TRUE STORY OF THE TEXAS CADET MURDER

PETER MEYER
Author of The Yale Murder

Nothing could come between high school sweethearts
Diane Zamora and David Graham—but something did:
beautiful blonde sophomore Adrianne Jones. After she and
Graham had a sexual encounter, a tearful Graham confessed everything to Zamora. Enraged and out-of-control,
Diane Zamora insisted that there was only one way to
restore the "purity" of their love . . . so together they
murdered Adrianne in an isolated spot outside of their
hometown of Mansfield, Texas. There were no suspects in
the murder until months later, when Diane confessed the
crime to her military school roommates, shocking friends,
family, and a picturesque Texas town . . .

**AVAILABLE WHEREVER BOOKS ARE SOLD
FROM ST. MARTIN'S PAPERBACKS**

Read the Edgar Award-winning true crime that will hold you spellbound...

TO THE LAST BREATH

Three Women Fight for the Truth Behind a Child's Tragic Murder

CARLTON STOWERS

Edgar Award-winning author of *Careless Whispers*

On April 22, 1994, two-year-old Renee Goode played happily with her sisters and cousin, as the four of them enjoyed an impromptu "slumber party" at the home of her father, Shane Goode. The next day she was dead. The medical examiner could not determine the cause of Renee's death, and the case was closed.

Only after Renee's mother, grandmother, and a gutsy female investigator fought to have the case re-examined, did the shocking truth emerge: cold-hearted Shane Goode had suffocated his tiny daughter to cash in on her death. Read this Edgar Award-winning account of that horrifying case—and of the bravery of three women seeking justice.

"Carlton Stowers has always been in the top rank of crime journalists. This is his best."
>   —Jack Olsen, author of *Hastened to the Grave*